DATE		

DATE DUE

Return Material Promptly

WHY
PEOPLE
PLAY

WHY
PEOPLE
PLAY

M. J. ELLIS

PRENTICE-HALL, INC., *Englewood Cliffs, New Jersey*

Library of Congress Cataloging in Publication Data

ELLIS, MICHAEL J
   Why people play.

   Bibliography:
      1.–Play. 2.–Leisure. 3.–Child study. I.–Title.
BF717.E43   155.5'18   72-6597
ISBN 0-13-958991-0

Printed in the United States of America

10 9 8 7 6 5

PRENTICE-HALL INTERNATIONAL, INC., *London*
PRENTICE-HALL OF AUSTRALIA, PTY. LTD., *Sydney*
PRENTICE-HALL OF CANADA, LTD., *Toronto*
PRENTICE-HALL OF INDIA PRIVATE LIMITED, *New Delhi*
PRENTICE-HALL OF JAPAN, INC., *Tokyo*

To
all those who
ask why people play
on learning what I do
I can now say,
"Read this book."

CONTENTS

PREFACE   xi

CHAPTER ONE

A PURVIEW OF THE PROBLEMS   1

Defining Play, 2   Managing Play, 2
Theorizing about Play, 4   Play as a Partner to Learning Technology, 4
Effects of Theory on Practice, 6

CHAPTER TWO

DEFINITIONS OF PLAY   9

The Meaning of the Word—Play, 10
Play Defined by Motive, 12   Play as Voluntary Behavior, 13
Intrinsic Motives for Play, 15
The Nature of Intrinsic Motivation, 16
Play Defined by Content, 17   Play as Undefinable, 20
Summary, 22

CHAPTER THREE

CLASSICAL THEORIES OF PLAY   23

The Nature of Theory, 24
Surplus Energy Theories of Play, 27

Play as Relaxation, 33
Relaxation and Surplus Energy Theory Reconciled, 35
Play as an Instinct, 36
Play as Preparation, 40   Play as Recapitulation, 42
Summary, 45

CHAPTER FOUR

RECENT THEORIES OF PLAY   49

Task Generalization and Compensation, 50
Cathartic Theories of Play, 54
Psychoanalytic Theory of Play, 57
Play Therapy, 61
Cognitive Dynamics and Play, 64
Play as Learned Behavior, 70   Overview, 76

CHAPTER FIVE

MODERN THEORIES OF PLAY   80

Neophilia and Neophobia, 81
Play as Stimulus-Seeking: History of the Idea, 83
Recent Research Thrusts, 85   The Neural Mechanisms of Arousal, 89
Stimulus Events and Impact, 91
A New Drive for Optimal Arousal, 93
Arousal Seeking Behaviors, 96   Epistemic Behavior, 99
Play and the Competence/Effectance Motive, 100
Boredom and Stereotyped Behavior, 104
Arousal Avoidance, 107   Redefinition of Play, 108

CHAPTER SIX

AN INTEGRATION   112

Play and Evolution, 113
The Inheritance of Capacity to Change, 114

Variability in Play, 116   Learning and Play, 116
Development—Inheritance and Experience, 117

CHAPTER SEVEN

IMPLICATIONS FOR PRACTICE   **119**

People at Work or Play, 120
Play in the Home, 127   Playthings, 134   Playgrounds, 137
Play with Others: Cooperation and Competition, 139
Adult Play, 141   Play and the Ill and Handicapped, 146
Concluding Comment, 147

REFERENCES   **149**

INDEX   **161**

PREFACE

This book is about the various answers to the questions, "What is play?" and "Why do people play?"

Awareness of the importance of play in the life of the child has grown to the point at which everyone concerned with the management of children pays at least lip service to it. Concern for play has been reawakened by the timely coincidence of several thrusts in our society. First, research has been done showing clearly that the playful behavior indulged in by the young is critical for their development. This was achieved in time to spur the massive attempts in the 1960s to influence the early development of the young children of the disadvantaged groups through programs like "Headstart." Headstart may have lost impetus, but the nation's appetite for early childhood education has been whetted, and it has been followed home by the proliferation of commercially provided opportunities for preschool experiences for the very young.

At the same time that commercial interests have been gearing-up for the provision of services to those who can purchase them, a lobby has grown up which is pressing for a universal child-development program for all children. This second pressure has been created by the desire of some to free mothers for work and of others to give women parity of opportunity with men, together with more enriching early experiences for their children outside the home. Playful behavior is seen as a desirable, if not the major, contribution to these experiences.

Paralleling this concern is the feeling in educational institutions that the process of formal education should be deformalized. There is a spirit moving the educational world which questions the appropriateness of some of its practices. There is an odious comparison between the behavior of many children as they learn what society prescribes and their behavior as they "play" with some elements of their environment. Education is coming to recognize that playful behavior is often motivated by an intense desire to learn that is accompanied by positive feelings of enjoyment, and much learning. The questions asked are old ones, "Can this be turned to our advantage?" and "Why don't we teach as the children seem to want to learn?"

Finally, a major trend that encompasses all. Increasingly we as a nation are concerned with the quality of our individual and collective lives. At last we are questioning the purposes of our democratic institutions, and our individual work. We are reaching agreement slowly that our social institutions exist to ensure highest possible quality of life for ourselves and countrymen. The puritan ethic that claims we live to work is beginning to be turned around so that we can agree that our political, judicial, and industrial systems exist to improve the quality of our lives; that we work to live. While hedonism is not in full flood, play and leisure are seen as the major resources for our achievement of individuality and they are beginning to receive the attention they have always deserved. Thus, the play of adults and children will become an increasingly critical area of concern and study as time passes.

This book is a small contribution to the thinking on play and leisure. It is designed to influence the provisions for play in the home, in the day-care or child development center, in the school, and in the provision of adult leisure services. However, play is an enormously complex subject and has been an enigma that has puzzled man since antiquity. This book bites off only one chewable chunk. It is a critical analysis of the content and assumptions of the many theories or explanations for play behavior.

The question, "Why do people play?" has been answered in many ways. Many of the answers have entered and continue to live in our culture influencing our attitudes toward play. We are embarking now, at an increasing pace, on attempts to actively plan for and thereby influence the play behavior of our peoples. It seems imperative to investigate the various explanations of why people play, because the answers clearly determine the provisions that are made. This book is about these various explanations. It then attempts to paint the implications that they have for the management of play in all its settings.

Where appropriate I have included the products of research already completed that bear on the topic at hand. This research is patchy; for example, the work on aggression is immense and I have contented myself with an investigation of the extant reviews, and yet there is almost no research on psychoanalytic theories of play. I am confident that all the theories of play have been included. However, I cannot be so confident that all the relevant research is included for two reasons. First, I had to find it and much probably slipped through my fingers. Second, once found, the relevance of a piece of research to an issue must be recognized and I may have failed to include it.

Now to warn you what to expect more directly. Chapter One is a brief overview of the problems inherent in attempting to manage play, and the arguments for and against. The second chapter is a necessary ground-clearing operation. Play has to be defined, at least *pro tem*, otherwise the interplay between author, reader, and the ideas cannot begin. Chapter Three analyzes the classical theories of play. These theories have in common their age and a concern with the inherent nature of play that was common across a species. They still influence much of our thinking today.

This treatment of the classical theories is followed by a chapter dealing with more recent explanations that have in common a recognition of the importance of preceding experiences of the individual player. The fifth chapter reviews in detail contemporary thinking on play and its motivations. The increased detail is necessary since the most up-to-date theory has an empirical base and seems best to explain playful behavior. Because it seems to have the greatest potential for upgrading practice and initiating worthy research it has been given most space. Each of the three substantive chapters are followed by a summarizing table giving the cause, assumptions, and criticisms of each theory. Of the last two chapters, six is an integration of three theories that together seem to hold most promise for explaining play, and seven takes the problems from the viewpoint of the practitioner sketching in principles of operation derived from Chapter Six.

The book was written while I was employed jointly by the Department of Mental Health of the State of Illinois' Adler Zone Center (AZC), and as a Research Assistant Professor in the Children's Research Center (CRC) and the Department of Leisure Sciences (DLS)—currently Department of Recreation and Park Administration but to change its name September 1, 1972—University of Illinois. The writing of the book became play for me since it was a respite from the pressures of my job as Director of the Motor Performance and Play Research Laboratory in the Children's Research Center. The laboratory and my activities were funded by the Department of Mental Health of the State of Illinois, the University of Illinois, and the National Institute of Mental Health, and was sponsored academically within the University of Illinois at Urbana-Champaign by the Department of Leisure Sciences. I am happy to acknowledge the support the troika of my superiors, Drs. Langan (AZC), Sapora (DLS) and Sprague (CRC), have given my work, one small part of which has been this book.

Many others helped me. Leslie Grover typed the manuscript and its drafts. Not only did she do this effectively but she also took an interest in the contents and my progress. Shirley Tewes, the Information Scientist for the Children's Research Center, creatively solved the problems of retrieving materials from the many libraries at the University of Illinois and elsewhere. My colleagues in the Motor Performance and Play Research Laboratory have all helped by getting the work of the laboratory done excellently, while I hid to write this book and I'm grateful. I am especially grateful for the germinal discussions that took place between Anthony Gramza, Anthony Linford, and myself in 1969. They led to my determination to write the book and stimulated a clearer conception of play as arousal-seeking. Since then I have had the benefits of constructive criticism from Joseph Bannon, Alan Sapora, Bernard Spodek, and Michael Wade, all of the University of Illinois. Finally, I acknowledge the contributions of the students that I have associated with in class and during research projects who, by their existence and questioning, were an omnipresent force for objectivity. I thank you all.

M. J. ELLIS
Champaign, Illinois

WHY
PEOPLE
PLAY

A PURVIEW
OF THE PROBLEMS

Chapter 1

The concept of the uniqueness and worth of each individual is a cornerstone in our culture. We espouse freedom from the coercion of ideology at the cognitive level, and from primary and acquired drives at the behavioral level. From this there follows a series of propositions that distill the essence of the American way of life. We believe individuals are important, and that each of us should be free to develop his own potential. These beliefs give rise to the notion that we should develop toward an increased heterogenization of our society. Differences between individuals should become greater as their unique potentials are better developed and, further, their behavior should become more different. Hence novel and creative responses are seen as desirable side effects of increasing concern with the unique rather than the stereotyped responses of an individual fulfilling external expectations. To the extent that we unfetter individuals from the demands of work or duty, we allow them leisure or opportunities to play and we commit those individuals to be themselves. Thus ideologically a human is most human, as defined by our culture, when at play.

Berlyne (1968) recognized this and wrote insightfully on the role of play and humor in the human condition. He said:

> Anyone who set out to design a human race without having met any specimens of the existing one might well see no reason why it could not conduct its daily business in deadly earnest. Yet almost all actual human societies appear to expend a great part of their time and energy in playful and humorous pursuits. It may be that all societies have their share of killjoys and spoilsports and prigs, but most of their members seem to prize opportunities for play and laughter and to appreciate other individuals who

1

make appropriate use of them. In our own society, those who devote themselves professionally to the provision of such opportunities are among the most lavishly remunerated and fulsomely idolized.

The apparent frivolity of play and humor should justify their receiving more, rather than less, investigation than other activities whose adaptive contributions are easy to understand. The very mysteries surrounding their function and the generous economic resources (four percent of the national income in the United States in 1959, according to De Grazia, 1962) that many, if not most, societies set aside for them, are strong reasons for giving a high priority to their study. As long as current theories have difficulty in accommodating these phenomena, we must infer that these theories have grave shortcomings and that it is urgently incumbent on us to remedy them [Berlyne, 1968, p. 796].

If play is important, it behooves us to come to grips with the factors that modulate play behavior and to manage them so that they facilitate rather than inhibit play.

Defining Play

There are several steps in the process of understanding play. The first step is to define play. The second is to establish the motives for and the content of play. The final step, and usually the reason for taking the first two, is to use the answers in the planning for play. This whole process is predicated on two assumptions. Firstly, that play is sufficiently important to warrant explaining and managing. Secondly, that it is behavior that is constrained by cause-effect relations and, therefore, can be explained and managed. Unfortunately these assumptions are not widely held, but they are necessary for this book.

Managing Play

Play is commonly considered to be the behavior emitted by an individual not motivated by the end product of the behavior. It is assumed to be free. The argument proceeds that if play is free, then to interfere with and manipulate it is to destroy its freedom and therefore its essential characteristic. This leads to a conclusion that play cannot be controlled or planned for and remain play.

This type of argument, however, cannot be sustained for long. Steinman (1970) has argued cogently that to consider play free is to assume arrogantly that we can control all the effects of our environment on behavior. For example, in classrooms we can assume that the behavior is controlled by teachers via the consequences they can control. The ebb and flow of contingencies and consequences within a formal classroom are relatively easy to disentangle and we can assume that they account for most of the behavior. However, if we remove the teachers, behavior will not become random or free of all constraints. There are hosts of other factors modulating the behavior of the child. Steinman sums up this situation:

> The idea of arranging free play may sound like a conflict of terms to many. Indeed a distinction is often made between free play and controlled or structured activity. Controlled play is not free play. However when this distinction is made, one wonders to whom the word "free" refers. Does "free" refer to the behavior of the playing child? Or does it refer to the lack of behavior of those designated by society to implement the child's socialization and education. When one frees himself from the task of controlling a child's behavior, he does not free the child. Instead he merely passes the controlling functions to others or the physical environment itself [Steinman, 1970, p. 6].

Play is under attack by the conditions of our modern world. In the life of the child the process of education has assumed critical importance and there has been a tendency for it to expand at the expense of play. Also, the urbanization and impaction of our society is tending to reduce the quality of life of our young and old alike. While the young still have leisure, and adults seem to be acquiring it, the essential designs of our lives are centered in setting the system appropriately for work, with other aspects planned for as an afterthought, if at all. Paradoxically, at the time when we stand a chance of achieving the temporal resources for leisure, it seems that these are being achieved at the expense of the other resources necessary for its worthwhile consumption.

Linder in his recent book *The Harried Leisure Class* (1970) refers to a development in our affluent society whereby time has become such an important commodity that even our leisure time is treated with attempts to make its use more efficient. Linder claims that we have started on the trend towards maximizing the economic efficiency of our leisure time by attending to the quantity of leisure experiences it encompasses. He goes on to develop the theme that the only really large period of uncommitted time is sleep, and even now there are signs of sleep being attacked systematically for the achievement of the individual's ends. He cites such attempts as subliminal learning during sleep, and the desire to make sleep more efficient, more refreshing, and so on.

Analogously, in the lives of our children, there is a period of apparently uncommitted time that is being sullied by similar incursions. Time spent playing represents a very large element in the child's profile of activities and represents a major opportunity for influencing the develop-

ment of the child. The tendency to exploit children's leisure began long
ago when Rousseau's fictitious program for the education of Emile was
published. Since then the rate and extent of imposition of goal-oriented
adult intervention has increased rapidly. At this time we see an intense
interest displayed by educators in utilizing the earlier, more plastic years
of the child to achieve their ends. The proliferation of preschools, nursery schools, day-care centers, head start programs, educational toys, and
television programs like "Sesame Street" all attest to the growing concern
for managing the behavior of children that falls outside the traditional
boundaries of the formal educational system. The boundary between
play and education is rapidly becoming blurred and many disparate
groups of professionals are concerned with the management of play.
There is an increasing concern for the management of play to achieve
goals judged worthy by the professionals concerned.

Theorizing about Play

The theorizing on play has proceeded sporadically since times of Classical Greece. With each new burst of interest in play the body of theory
has been evaluated in the light of the thinking of the times. A new burst
of theoretical activity is upon us, accompanying the increase in practical
concern for play. It is time to bring the record up to date again with
a critical evaluation of the potential explanations for play in order that
the current flowering of interest in managing play in the best interests of
the player can be based on sound explanations.

What is needed is an understanding of what sets play apart from non-
play, and a knowledge of the factors influencing play behavior. When
that is achieved our collective and individual planning for play can nurture the behavior rather than hazard it. We need a technology that will
permit those dealing with play to make adequate preparations for its
nurturance.

Play as a Partner to Learning Technology

A similar technology has been built from the psychology of learning
and can serve as an example. A major subdivision of psychological theory
has been devoted to establishing the laws describing the relationships
between the conditions existing before the emission of a response, the
response itself, and the events that arise as a consequence. An extremely
powerful law has been derived which, in its simplest form, says that responses that are followed closely by changes in the environment that
reward the individual have a higher probability of being emitted again,

when the antecedent conditions are similar. The response will be emitted with higher frequency if the results of the response are reinforcing. This simple concept, of course much elaborated in the various theories, has led to a revolution in the management of the behavior of not only lower animals but also humans. The concept has existed in an inchoate form since man started to interact with man, but the potential for producing change in the behavior of others was not realized until its underlying principles were clearly understood. There is now an extensive body of knowledge used by those concerned with managing others called behavior modification.

Behavior modification is merely a persistent procedure for maximizing the probability of desired responses occurring, and minimizing the probability of undesired responses. It is used deliberately with children with behavior problems or who are retarded and have failed to learn the prized skills that allow them to move freely in our society. This technology, now taught and used extensively in America, is in the main concerned with rigging the consequences or contingencies within an environment to pressure the child consistently towards emitting the appropriate or desired behaviors. Rigging the contingencies usually involves showing that obvious rewards like food and subtle rewards like smiles or other social reinforcements, are consistently differentially applied to responses that progressively approximate the desired behavior.

Behavior modification is a technique which holds promise for the control of those behaviors falling directly under the control of primary drives such as the need for food, shelter, and sex or the acquired drives in which the animal exhibits a need for social recognition, a smile, the opportunity to cuddle. In other words, behavior modification seems a powerful tool for those concerned with managing behavior controlled by reinforcing contingencies that are intrinsic to the organism. There remains, however, a major set of behaviors, play, which are not amenable to control by behavior modification without distorting their essential characteristics. The other set is, of course, that motivated and controlled by reinforcing contingencies which are not subject to control by an agency outside the organism. The responses from this subset of behaviors can be brought under the control of an extrinsic reward system, i.e., can be produced at will by the attachment of a reinforcing contingency that is consistently applied, but by so doing the very nature of the response is altered. It becomes extrinsically rather than intrinsically motivated. An essential ingredient for normal human behavior is that some behavior be intrinsically motivated. All those behaviors emitted because of curiosity in what will happen, a desire to create a new response, and the manipulation of the environment just because it is there are essentially intrinsically motivated responses.

What is missing in the armamentarium of our behavioral techniques is a sister technology to that of behavior modification which will allow us to plan for, and manage, intrinsically motivated behavior.

While behavior modification has been growing in stature and power there have been few attempts to integrate the current thinking on the factors controlling the emission of intrinsically motivated responses into a similar technology. The thought of creating an arid technology for the rigid control of play behavior may be horrifying. However, it is only horrifying because those concerned with its management have hitherto not considered that their unwillingness to intrude into the play situation did not remove a host of subtle contingencies which themselves were manipulating the behavior. Failure to understand and control the subtle factors that interact with the intrinsic motivations of the organism relinquishes managerial responsibility to chance.

Behavior modification, then, might best be described as a procedure for ensuring that the child possesses the battery of responses required of him for entry into the culture. The sister technology would be concerned with the provision of opportunities for the child to develop his own unique characteristics and to develop a capacity to create new responses and solutions to his own problems.

Play behavior seems to occur when sufficient contingencies to responding are suspended to allow intrinsic motives to sustain behavior. Thus, by this definition, play would seem to fall beyond the ambit of behavior modification. In the absence of positive and negative contingencies, be they dependent on primary or acquired drives, the behavior of the organism becomes less oriented toward specific goals. It becomes more diffuse and reflects its individuality.

Effects of Theory on Practice

Several things must happen before a play theory can be as influential in practice as the Law of Effect has been in its sphere, via behavior modification. First, the researchers and practitioners in the area must be awakened to the benefits of good theory and the shortcomings of existing theory. The problem must be identified. The current lack of critical analysis in the realm of motivation to play is startling by its absence. Play, or at least free-ranging activity, is an extensive behavioral category, yet researchers have shown little theoretical concern. Practitioners continue either to base their work on the outmoded theories that abound in the field or to adopt an atheoretical approach. The problem is clear. There is little or no satisfactory body of theory concerning the motive to play, and hence what play really is, existing in the minds of those making decisions influencing the play behavior of our people. Practitioners and researchers alike are behaving as if they existed in a pretheoretic phase, when there does seem to be a satisfactory body of theory waiting to guide them.

The problem is to sensitize those concerned with play to the contribution a satisfactory theory of behavior can make to their thinking regarding the phenomena in which they are interested. Research, unless it involves a fishing trip to "determine the effects of . . . ," must move from a theoretical position. It is not enough to describe what happens; science is greater than that. The major effort should be placed on answering the question why something happens. Practice is elevated from an art form to the extent that practitioners can explain why they are doing what they do to reach a given goal. If it is based on a theoretical underpinning, practice can be explained, communicated, and evaluated.

Ironically, in this area of play behavior there are many theories. This book deals with the 15 that have been advanced. Most of them have serious logical shortcomings or are not substantiated by empirical findings. Despite clear weaknesses, however, there has been an unquestioning acceptance, or perhaps tolerance, of these theories by most people concerned with play. The tragedy is that lately we have not been concerned with a critical questioning of the tenets of the various theories. Researchers have not sought empirical evidence of the theories' validity, and practitioners have not critically examined the value of the various theories in explaining or predicting the behavior of their clients. For those in recreation, preschool and elementary education, child development, architecture, landscape architecture, the question "why do people play?" would seem to be a critical one.

The second stage in the process of sensitization must be to give those concerned with the play of people insights into a critical analysis of the traditional theories of play. Their shortcomings must be presented. Practitioners should have as healthy a skepticism as researchers concerning the guidelines for their actions. In general, the theories that have traditionally been invoked to explain play have sufficient shortcomings to be of little use. However, old theories do not just die. They linger on and can only be eliminated from the sphere of influence by a process of rejection. They remain as contaminants of our thinking unless we take care to eliminate them. Their shortcomings need to be displayed for all to see.

The third stage in the process must be to present a more powerful alternative. The best theory is the one that explains the data and experience (experience is a kind of data) concerning the phenomenon and most accurately predicts future outcomes. In the absence of a better theory, the one we have is best. Fortunately, there has emerged a powerful explanation for play that grows from several streams of research done since World War II. Unfortunately, this theory currently rests gently in the world of academe and has not been moved to the point where it is guiding research and practice in the fields concerned with play. It needs to be paraded alongside the older theories to compete for the privilege of guiding action.

The fourth stage must be to suggest some ways in which this approach should influence practice and research. Examples of the implications that this approach has for the allied fields of research and practice are needed to sensitize those concerned to its benefits.

There are many barriers to a general recognition of the problems associated with each of the 4 stages we must pass through to rationalize our understanding and management of play. However, the situation is not hopeless. Currently there exists an atmosphere of concern for play, and the purpose of this book is to exploit that concern and to take the reader through the 4 stages necessary for a better understanding of play.

DEFINITIONS OF PLAY

In English play has many meanings. The word has been taken into many facets of the language to imply activity that is usually pleasant and voluntary. The subset of meanings we are concerned with in this book is that which is used in common parlance to describe activities that are not serious; that are indulged in a playful manner. The meanings are those ascribed to the word in the common usage of the word in statements such as "the kids are playing" or "come and play." In common parlance the meaning is clearly understood. What is also important is that the activities that are playful can easily be discriminated by most people, even in other species. That which makes for playfulness can be easily recognized by humans in chimps, dogs, whales, and other species and most probably individuals of these species can reverse the process and recognize some playful responses in man. Since we can in large measure agree, play should be easy to define. However, it has proved a puzzle for centuries.

To many, play denotes behavior which is trivial, fruitless, not under the control of known contingencies. These persons frequently refer to some segments of children's behavior as "just play." But to characterize such behavior from the observer's viewpoint is dangerous. The evidence is mounting fast that "just playing" is a crucial ingredient in the development of at least the higher mammals.

Play as a word describing behavior seems to set aside a class or complex of behaviors that to some are fruitless, to others a class of behaviors deriving from a motive, and to others a subset of behaviors whose unifying essence is that the contingencies maintaining the behavior are not easy to detect. The first and last concepts have much in common in that they depict behavior play as apparently nonproductive; they differ only in that the lay view makes a value judgment about the worth of the activities. A judgment that is wrong.

The question then is to decide what is play. What motivates it, and what benefits does it work. When these questions are answered we will have at hand the knowledge to maximize its benefits.

The Meaning of the Word—Play

Huizinga (1949) devotes a whole chapter to the history of the word "play" in language. The word has taken on a great many meanings in the Occidental and Oriental languages he analyzed. In some tongues there is just one word to describe all play activities, and in others there are special words to describe the separate activities. In English we have both a general descriptor, "play," and a host of other words to describe the various activities we use as play. In each language there have developed the words necessary to enable its speakers to communicate the concepts of play that were extant in their culture. Huizinga's analysis stands above what is necessary here, but it exemplifies, by its very etymological complexity, the complexity of our human conceptions of the nature of play.

The Huizinga analysis reveals that man, particularly Western man, has wrestled with the problem of defining play in two ways. At times we have needed a term to include all the behaviors that comprise play, and to induce into our experiences of playful behaviors the common element that sets them apart. On other occasions we have wished to describe particular activities that are playful but are separable from one another under the general rubric of play. This need has stemmed from the recognition that play is a multitude of behaviors. These two streams of thinking which either try to define the common differentiating elements that set play apart or attempt to develop ways of handling the variety of behaviors by giving each its own word, have recently been joined by a third. This school of thought feels we have been led astray by our persistent attempt to categorize everything neatly into mutually excluding sets with their own names. The third school denies that behaviors can be differentiated simply into the two sets of play and not play. The enigma arises from the structure of our language (Kelly, 1958).

Huizinga deals with our tendency to split categories into exclusive opposite sets. Thus, a layman will frequently define play as "not-work." Play becomes merely all the behavior that is left outside the realm of work. Although this definition is not satisfying, it seems to have some truth. Play as a complex of behaviors is categorized by this definition as nonproductive or apparently not instrumental in the process of survival.

Play clearly has this element in that it is preempted by the need to emit behaviors which ensure survival, and this notion runs reliably through most of the definitions of play that have been handed down to us (Sapora & Mitchell, 1961).

In societies with a strong streak of puritanism, play, by virtue of being unrelated to survival, production and profit, stood outside and inferior to the processes of work. This attitude is still strong. The word "just" is regularly added to "play" to indicate that the behavior is not only noncritical but also trivial.

Huizinga juxtaposed play not with work but with the word "earnest."

> The conceptual value of a word is always conditioned by the word which expresses its opposite. For us, the opposite of play is *earnest,* also used in the more special sense of *work;* while the opposite of earnest can either be play or jesting, joking. However, the complementary pair of opposites *play-earnest* is the more important.
>
> We can say, perhaps, that in language the play-concept seems to be much more fundamental than its opposite. The need for a comprehensive term expressing "not-play" must have been rather feeble, and the various expressions for "seriousness" are but a secondary attempt on the part of language to invent the conceptual opposite of "play." They are grouped round the ideas of "zeal," "exertion," "painstaking," despite the fact that in themselves all these qualities may be found associated with play as well [Huizinga, 1949, pp. 44–45].

Linguistically, play presents a problem. Our propensity for exclusive categories leads us astray. "Playful-earnest" adverbs, or "play-work" verbs, are not necessarily antithetical.

> . . . we find that the two terms are not of equal value: play is positive, earnest negative. The significance of "earnest" is defined by and exhausted in the negation of "play"—earnest is simply "not playing" and nothing more. The significance of "play," on the other hand, is by no means defined or exhausted by calling it "not-earnest," or "not serious." Play is a thing by itself. The play-concept as such is of a higher order than is seriousness. For seriousness seeks to exclude play, whereas play can very well include seriousness [Huizinga, 1949, p. 45].

Most English language definitions of play till now have been based on the assumption that there is a definable subset of behavior which is play and that this subset can be defined in terms of its common and discriminating elements. We have searched for the neat paradigm to categorize simply our behavior into work and play even though work activities can be carried out playfully and play can appear serious. At the same time

English has developed many words to describe the particular activities, both motor and cognitive, that are indulged in playfully or without earnestness. We have not yet found a way to label play as an exclusive category. The difficulty may merely lie in our need to balance·"work" as a category in our symbolism.

There are two distinct threads running through the various definitions. While it is possible to separate these distinct threads, most definitions intertwine them. One thread running through most definitions can be identified as a notion that play can be discriminated in terms of the motive of the player. The other attempts to discriminate by means of the attributes of the play behavior itself. Beach (1945) established the requirements for this. "Any serviceable definition of play must be based upon a number of predominating characteristics which combine to set it off from non-playful behavior [p. 539]." The first thread, depending on the motive, requires the imputation of that motive by the observer. The second requires the careful analysis of the attributes of play and assumes that there are common discriminants that set it apart.

Play Defined by Motive

The oldest definitions are those based on a particular theory. Play behavior is defined in terms of its assumed cause or motive. This class of definitions have the general form "Play is the behavior motivated by 'x,' where 'x' is the presumed motive. Providing there exists a method for detecting the presence of 'x' or making objective descriptions of the conditions when 'x' is produced, then play can be defined. Given the required situation and the assumed motive, play is the behavior produced."

Thus, for each theory concerning the motive for play it is possible to create a definition that follows the general form. Several examples of this type of definition are mentioned by Sapora and Mitchell (1961, p. 114). Schiller is cited as defining play as "the aimless expenditure of exuberant energy." According to this definition, play is created by the existence of surplus energy. Thus, to define play, the motive, the existence of a specific kind of energy, surplus energy, must be determinable. Further, the behavior expending it must be aimless in the eyes of the beholder. The difficulty is not resolved by such a definition. The problem is merely passed along the sentence to a definition of motive.

Another example cited by Sapora and Mitchell (1961, p. 114) was Groos's 1898 definition of play as "instinctive practice, without serious intent, of activities that will later be essential to life." Here the definition stems directly from Groos's attempt to explain the motive for play by making the assumption that even if the play were not serious or critical at the moment it had significance as practice for later life. Since Groos did not wish to make the assumption that the animal could foresee what would be the critical responses in the future, he added instincts to motivate the behavior appropriately. Hall is cited as defining play as the "motor habits and spirit of the past persisting in the present." Hall believed that play was merely a process whereby the young animal playfully recapitulated activities which were critical for the survival of the race earlier in its history. Acceptance of these definitions depends on an acceptance of the original theory from which they were derived. They are not really definitions of what play is, but statements of belief about why play occurs. Further analysis of these theories of motivation to play is required before judgment can be passed on such definitions.

Play as Voluntary Behavior

A variant on the general form of the definition of play behavior in terms of its motive sustains many definitions that claim play to be behavior which is not-motivated, or voluntary. The behavior occurs in the absence of motives as imputed by the observer. Since the observer cannot perceive why the subject is behaving, it is assumed that the subject is playing.

However, it is dangerous to assume that the motive for the individual behavior can be imputed by an observer. Schlosberg (1947) points out that the motives are frequently obscure and that without the opportunity to manipulate the situation the evidence on which the observer makes the inference is flimsy.

> For example, the male Siamese Fighting Fish (*Betta splendens*) will desert the bubble nest containing eggs if the temperature drops a few degrees. Or he may carry out other partial activities, such as building the nest but not mating with the female, if the diet has been inadequate. Presumably hormonal and neural factors are of great importance, but they have not been studied adequately in this species. Do we understand these partial patterns better if we say "The male is only playing at breeding?" [Schlosberg, 1947, p. 230].

Thus, Schlosberg draws our attention to the fact that much of our definition of play depends simply on the fact that we cannot perceive why the animal is behaving. It boils down to simply stating that play is play because one cannot see what utility the behavior has for the animal. It is play because one thinks it is not work.

To take a definition of this kind as an example, Huizinga says of play:

> . . . we might call it free activity standing quite consciously outside "ordinary" life as being "not serious," but at the same time absorbing the player intensely and utterly. It is an activity connected with no material interest and no profit can be gained by it [Huizinga, 1949, p. 13].

Thus, play is voluntary, absorbing activity that is not critical or does not contribute to survival. These two elements must be derived from the same notion that critical responses are not voluntary in the sense that the animal must emit them to survive. At bottom then the definition rests on the imputation by the observer of whether the behavior is critical or not. Huizinga does not specify why the behavior is emitted nor does he describe the ingredients of play other than to state that they are absorbing.

The concept of voluntary behavior, freedom to emit the playful responses or not, is the major determinant in the following set of definitions cited by Sapora and Mitchell (1961) which exemplify many of the definitions and capture the sense of the layman's definition:

> Lazarus—Play is activity which is itself free, aimless, amusing or diverting.
> Dewey—Activities not consciously performed for the sake of any result beyond themselves.
> Gulick—What we do because we want to do it.
> Stern—Play is voluntary self-sufficient activity.
> Patrick—Those human activities which are free and spontaneous and which are pursued for their own sake. Interest in them is self-sustaining, and they are not continued under any internal or external compulsion.
> Rainwater—Play is a mode of behavior, . . . involving pleasurable activity of any kind, not undertaken for the sake of reward beyond itself. . . .
> Pangburn—Activity carried on for its own sake [Sapora & Mitchell, 1961, p. 114.]

All these definitions and the multitudes like them claim that play is not motivated by any other motive than seeking the reward inherent immediately in the activity itself. The activity is seen as rewarding of itself without reference to the primary motives of survival. In other words, it is easy to beg the question of what causes the playful behavior by claiming that either play as a category is intrinsically motivating or each particular activity is.

Intrinsic Motives for Play

To postulate an intrinsic motive for an activity without establishing its nature and mechanism is merely to claim that because there is a behavior there must be a motive and it is that motive which drives the behavior. This unsatisfactory thinking led to the proliferation of instincts as motives that hampered our understanding of the causes of behavior during the early part of the century and which is dealt with in detail in Chapter 3. Saying a set of behaviors is intrinsically motivating begs the question and leaves open how the activity is motivated, and whether there is one common motive for all intrinsically satisfying behaviors or a special motive for each behavior.

The crucial question thus becomes what is intrinsically motivating about the activities indulged in during playful behavior. The answer can set off in different directions. It is possible to advance the answer that the behavior is spontaneous, unmotivated, having no cause. Alternatively, each intrinsically motivating activity can be assumed to have its own particular motive, or some common intrinsic motive can be seen to sustain all play behaviors.

The first answer requires us to reject a basic tenet of science, that events obey some finite causation. The second leads to the old trap of listing a motive for each activity; of revisiting the instinct (motive) naming of yore. The final explanation is the only one that can sustain an attempt at understanding the phenomenon.

Assuming that the motive for play is intrinsic, that is, inherent in the process of the interaction itself, while extrinsically motivated behavior is sustained by the need to achieve some goal, it should be possible to differentiate play behavior from extrinsically motivated need reduction. There seem to be two ways of separating these classes of motives.

The simplest, which applies only to humans at this time, is to ask the subjects why they behaved as they did. The answers need careful management if they are really to contribute to our understanding. A host of intervening variables of a social nature cloud the issue even if the subject really does know why he is doing something.

Alternatively, the contingencies or consequences of the behavior can be manipulated. If the behavior is only sustained by the goal or reward, the removal of the reward will eliminate the behavior. If the behavior continues, then presumably there is another reward. The reward may be intrinsic to the behavior or it may be of course that there is some other hitherto undiscovered contingency in the setting maintaining the behavior. In theory, therefore, the presence of intrinsically motivated behavior, play, could be detected if the behavior continued when the intrinsic contingencies were eliminated. Thus, if the behavior in question ceased on the elimination of extrinsic motivation, the behavior could be classified, post hoc, as work or non-play.

The difficulty in this lies in the necessary assumption that all extrinsic contingencies have been identified and eliminated. To discriminate this way would require extensive analysis of the contingencies operating and the experimental manipulation of the situation. Such an experiment would allow post hoc decisions that might be of use in research, but the size of the task would render it impractical in the clinical setting. However, as a concept, it allows a theoretical or conceptual view of what is play. In the practical management of play the concept per se allows persons with insight and personal knowledge of the situation to be analyzed to make a better judgment of what is play. With this definition play situations can either be recognized more easily, or be freed more effectively from limiting extrinsic contingencies. This process is dealt with more extensively in Chapter 7—"Implications for Practice."

The Nature of Intrinsic Motivation

What is the nature of the intrinsic motivation that energizes and directs the playful behavior of animals? The answer to this question will allow us to define play in terms of the motive. The definition will take on the general form "Play is the behavior that is intrinsically motivated." Providing there exists an explicit method for detecting the presence of 'x', or making objective descriptions of the condition that produces 'x', then the behavior produced can be operationalized. The motive is inferred from descriptions of what occurred before the behavior and the behavior itself.

Recently such explicit definitions have begun to appear. For example, Barnett defined exploration "as any behavior which tends to increase the rate of change in the stimulation falling on the animals' receptors which is not impelled by homeostatic need [1963, p. 26]." Rewriting in the general form, this becomes "Play is the behavior motivated by the need to increase the rate of change of stimulation." Hunt defines the intrinsic motivation as, ". . . motivation inherent in the organism's informational interaction with circumstances through the distance receptors. . . . [1965, p. 197]." While these definitions do not answer all the problems, they do lead logically to the variety of behaviors which produce the stimulus changes or informational interactions.

These behaviors have been categorized as the investigation, exploration, and manipulation of the physical, social, and cognitive environ-

ments. These categories seem to describe facets of what is generally
assumed to be play. The preceding definitions are derived from the idea
that the motive which sustains these behaviors is arousal-seeking. Thus,
fitting the definition to the general form, it becomes, "play is the behavior
motivated by the need to avoid boredom and maintain arousal."

Enough definitions that are derived directly from motivational constructs and having the form "Play is the behavior motivated by 'x' " have
been dealt with here for the reader to recognize them. Their value depends directly on the definition of the motive. The elegance and power
of the many explanations of the motives for or causes of play behavior
varies considerably. The process of selecting a definition of play having
the general form must depend on the selection of the most powerful
causal explanation. This process of selecting a definition that depends
on a definition of the motive must be deferred until the rival explanations for the behavior have been considered.

Play Defined by Content

The second thread twining through some definitions is that play can
be defined in terms of its content. It is assumed that if laymen, and
presumably other animals, can differentiate play from non-play then it
should be possible to write down the attributes of the animal, its behavior, and the setting which signal the playful character of play behavior.

Ethologists have shown considerable interest in play. Their modus
operandi is well suited to the task of dealing satisfactorily with such
subtle distinctions as what is or is not play. Their approach is a holistic
one, taking into account the complex interactions between the behavior
of the animal and its surroundings. A fundamental premise of ethology
is that removing an animal from its naturalistic surroundings so disturbs
its behavior that there is a risk that it will bear little relation to its normal
or natural behavior.

The ethologist's approach is to observe long sequences of behavior un-
obtrusively, carefully classifying the relations between items of behavior
and the setting. These relations are carefully analyzed to try to determine
the chains of antecedent-subsequent events or to infer the cause-effect
relations that exist in the natural setting. The complex analysis of behaviors and their interactions is the raw material from which the ethological study of animal behavior proceeds.

The ethological approach, with its heavy emphasis on the observation
of what actually happens, has led to definitions of play that depend on
its content. Poole (1966) studied carefully a subclass of play behaviors,
aggressive play, emitted by polecats. His work involved analyzing a group

of behaviors that he recognized as play among polecats. The analysis dealt with the development of this behavior in young polecats, its characteristics in adults, and of course the differences between real and play aggression.

Poole concluded that there were many attributes of aggressive play which discriminated it from real aggression. Aggressive play was goal-less in the sense that it was not directed towards the normal goal for aggression. The discomfiture of the retaliator was not pursued. The playful behavior was obviously make-believe in that the aggressor clearly limited the vigor of his play attack to the vigor of the retaliation. There was no striving for a rapid and clear resolution of the behavior and the aggressor was careful to avoid the establishment of clear and discomfiting superiority in order to allow the behavior to continue.

The behavior consisted of adult aggressive patterns that were ritualized. They were not modified and refined as a result of experience to achieve their goal more efficiently. The behavior was apparently pleasant since it could be directed towards an unresponsive animal or object. Finally, the behavior was reduced or preempted by stimuli in the environment that stimulated goal-directed activity. In summary, therefore, aggressive play in polecats is normally goal-directed activity that appears out-of-context in an unmodifiable and incomplete form. It is ritualized and pleasant and preempted by goal-directed activity.

While this descriptive definition appeared as a result of the study of just one kind of behavior, it bears a remarkable similarity to Loizos' (1966) definition derived from a review of the ethologically oriented works on the subject. She concluded that "Playful acts are motor behaviors that are divorced from their usual motivation and are qualitatively distinct from the same patterns appearing in their originally motivated contexts [p. 7]." She went on to specify in what way they were qualitatively distinct. Transference to a playful context resulted in:

1. reordering of the sequences of the acts,
2. repetition of some of the items more often than would occur normally,
3. exaggeration of some items, and
4. fragmentation and incompletion of some items or sequences.

The result is inefficient in the sense that the normal life-support goals are not achieved.

Beach as long ago as 1945 outlined the essential characteristics of play.

(1) It is commonly stated or implied, although it can not be objectively demonstrated, that playful behavior in animals as in man carries an emotional element of pleasure. Not all pleasant activities are playful; but all

play is assumed to be pleasurable. (2) Play is usually regarded as characteristic of the immature animal rather than the adult. Grown individuals may play; but they do so less frequently than juvenile members of their species. (3) It is usually supposed that play differs from non-playful responses in having no relatively immediate biological result which affects the continued existence of the individual or the species. In other words, play is customarily regarded as non-utilitarian. (4) The outward forms of play are relatively species-specific. Dogs play in certain ways, horses in others, and apes in still others. (5) The amount, duration and diversity of play in a given species is related to its phylogenetic position. In general, play is more frequent, more variable, and occurs during a longer portion of the life span in higher animals than in lower. The play of fishes appears infrequent and stereotyped when compared with that of lower mammals; while the play of dogs is less diversified and prolonged than that of monkeys and apes [Beach, 1945, p. 524].

Little effort seems to have been applied to producing similar statements concerning the characteristics of human play. Perhaps this is simply because, as Beach alludes in his fifth point, the general characteristics of all play are similar and apply to humans. There are species-specific patterns but these patterns or contents fit within the general statement. The general trend is for more diversified and sustained play behavior as the species themselves become more complex. Thus, the play of humans, the most highly diversified and complex animals, would seem to have specific elements that are unique to the species, to the race, and to the individual. Yet that behavior is still described by the list of general characteristics.

Based upon the preceding principles, it is presumed that, via a description of the behavior in a naturalistic setting, play behaviors of any animal can be differentiated from non-play activity. The process can be applied to any species but it requires lengthy observation and considerable skill to code the behavioral events in fine enough detail to produce the necessary discriminants.

The application of a naturalistic approach to the behavior of children is exemplified by the work of Hutt (1966), Blurton-Jones (1967; 1972a,b,c; in press), and Leach (1972) in England. In the United States the approach has been similar in method and content but has been identified with workers clustering around Barker (1951, 1955, 1963, 1968) at the University of Kansas. The outcomes of their work has not in general led to much theorizing in the classical sense, but has produced excellent descriptions of the content of children's play.

For example, Gump, Schoggen, and Redl (1963) describe fully the play of a young boy in two different settings: at home and in camp. They claim that play for their subject was comprised of watching, sensual en-

joyment, reading, manipulative amusement, investigation and exploration, stunts, unorganized sport, roughhousing, informal and formal active
games, stationary games, construction, verbal joking, teasing, and dra-
matics.

The extraordinary richness of the behavior of their subject, Wally
O'Neill, during play exemplified the problem of reducing the structure of
play of humans to some simple statement or construct.   Poole's analysis
of the play-fighting of polecats could be applied to the roughhousing
activities of Wally O'Neill directly.   However, many other categories
appeared in this particular child's play, each of which would presumably
require analysis.   Wally O'Neill's play also differed somewhat from home
to camp, thereby further complicating the issue.

Hutt (1966) identified the course of play behavior of nursery school
children in a much more constrained setting.   The children were given a
novel, red, box-like device with a lever.   The lever would make the box
emit sounds and increase the value of digital counters according to its
movement.   By manipulating the complexity of the consequences of the
lever's movement, the complexity of the box could be controlled.

The course of the behavior followed stages, in which there was first
exploration, then manipulation.   Finally, the child moved to a kind of
behavior that Hutt called "transposition of function."   Here the child
incorporated the box into other activities.   This behavior was most like
what a lay person would call play.

The nature of the problem is clearly exemplified by the differences
between the two studies.   Gump, Schoggen, and Redl (1963) tried to observe the stream of the behavior of their subject in natural settings.   The
outcome was a bewildering array of responses and the authors were justi-
fiably proud of having developed a system for handling data of such
complexity.   Unfortunately, the specificity of the outcome was high.   The
description just seemed to fit Wally O'Neill at home and at camp.   Hutt
(1966), on the other hand, studied a set of responses of a group of children to a specific and limited situation—play with an unusual red box
under carefully controlled conditions.

Hutt's finer grained analysis seemed to hold more potential for the
production of generalizable statements about the motive for play in general.   She described the content of play on the way to some specific
empirical tests of a theory concerning play, whereas the Gump paper
seemed content merely to chart the course of the behavior.

Play as Undefinable

The remaining view holds that the traditional process of defining play
is counter-productive.   The behavior it attempts to include in one cate-

gory is not an exclusive one.   It includes bodily activities involving objects, and members of the players and other species, games, and sports. The sheer heterogeneity of this mélange of activities that can be broken down into a variety of categories such as investigation, manipulation, specific and diverse exploration, and epistemic behavior, seems to preclude the possibility of arriving at general principles predicting the nature, occurrence, and setting of all these behaviors (Hutt, 1966).

Millar (1968) makes the same point.   "The gallant attempts to provide direct, comprehensive theories of play are inadequate partly because they attempt to define and treat play as an activity with a common core and with characteristics that distinguish it from all others [p. 21]."

Play is not completely distinct from non-play or work.   It is easy to imagine a setting in which the play of the individual also serves some productive function.   When a man is both playing and working, how do we classify the behavior?   Millar (1968) again proposes a solution.   "Perhaps play is best used as an adverb; not as a name of a class of activities, nor as distinguished by the accompanying mood but to describe how and under what conditions an action is performed [p. 21]."

Behaviors then are defined not as play, but playful.   By so doing the problems inherent in partitioning human behavior into work and play are eliminated and we are left with the problem of discriminating playful from non-playful activities.   Lieberman (1965, 1966) attempted this differentiation for humans.   She hypothesized that there were relationships between creativity, divergent thinking, and playfulness.   To test this hypothesis she had to define and quantify playfulness as a personality trait in her subjects—kindergartners.   She rated quantity and quality of physical, social and cognitive spontaneity, manifest joy, and sense of humor and predicted that these were in fact the expressions of one personality trait—playfulness.   Her factor analysis of these five measures supported her prediction and so a definition of playfulness was born.   Playful behavior is the kind of behavior emitted by playful children.   Playful children were creative divergent thinkers who were spontaneous in their physical, social and cognitive behaviors, were manifestly joyful emitting many expressions of delight, liking, smiling and chuckling, and exhibited a sense of humor by teasing or, as Lieberman put it, "glint-in-the-eye" behavior.   These behaviors must have been operationally defined in the original study to allow them to be rated.   However, her writings suggest a flavor of flexibility, a willingness to step outside the convention and to generate new experiences rather than to be content to move in lockstep with the interplay stimulus-response-stimulus.   Lieberman goes on to answer questions concerning the development and stability of this trait, but she has left us with some data and a definition of playfulness in the behavior of children.

Summary

The perplexing problem of how to define play will only be resolved by continually regenerating new definitions that fit current concepts of play behavior. The organization of the chapter reflects the general solutions to the problem currently in vogue. Play can be defined in terms of its motive or its content.

Both types of definition require effort on the part of the persons seeking the definition. If the seekers prefer the general form "Play is the behavior motivated by 'x'," then they must accept the necessity for formulating a motive or theory for play. If they prefer to define play by content, then they must recognize the need for extensive observation. Most laymen have observed enough play behavior to discriminate it from earnest behavior and so can make subjective decisions. However, if they wish to describe the behavior objectively, or to explain exactly how they are making the discrimination, then they must be prepared for a lengthy process of careful observation and analysis.

Finally, some have given up hope, claiming that play is indefinable; that it is in the best interest of all to recognize the heterogeneity of play behaviors and deal with them separately. The only unifying suggestion from this third school is that perhaps play is only play because it is playful. This approach does not concern itself with the contents but with the attributes of play behavior. It is closely allied to the content approach and deals with the elements of the behavior that signals "this response is playful."

Play, then, is a plastic construct which has yet to be satisfactorily operationalized in a way that satisfies all.

CLASSICAL THEORIES
OF PLAY

Chapter 3

Many theories have been advanced to explain play. Each has in some way reflected the spirit of its times and had some explanatory power at the time of its formulation. These theories can be categorized as classical and recent (Gilmore, 1966a), and contemporary. This chapter deals with the classical theories.

The classical theories were advanced originally before the turn of this century, although in some cases there have been more recent elaborations. There are five classical theories of play. Four of the theories can be aligned in two pairs, each of which predicts opposite outcomes given the same circumstances. The fifth is the theory that play is instinctive. The first pair concerned the energy expenditure of the organism. One explained play as the mandatory release of surplus energy created by efficient or societal provision for life support. The other saw play as relaxing activity called forth to dissipate the effects of previous stressful and/or aversive activities that were necessary for survival. These two theories obviously predict opposite behavior under the same circumstances.

Providing a link between the pairs is the simplest view; play is an instinct. Instincts are inherited, or at least preexistent tendencies to behave in a given way. Play was seen as a preexistent tendency to emit behavior when none of the other more powerful or pre-potent instincts were at work.

In the remaining pair, play on the one hand is seen as behavior that practices instinctive responses of the species in preparation for adulthood, and on the other, play is viewed as the instinctive recapitulation of the critical responses emitted during the development of the race or species. Both of these theories emerged during the era of the instinct and were derived from the view that behavior was instinctive.

These five classical theories were concerned with those elements in the nature of man in general that lead him to play, and with the purposes play serves. The particular responses that comprise play were not accounted for. It was sufficient that the organism was behaving but not working. The theories did not take into account individual differences and were in the main armchair theories. They have lingered on in our literature and thinking and, although they were amenable to testing, they have spawned little research.

In contrast, recent theories are concerned with the individual and his behavior, attempting to explain the differences among the play of individuals. In these theories the recent experiences of the individual are seen as the antecedent events conditioning the emitted behavior and they are concerned essentially with the content of play. Classical theories attempt to explain why play exists, whereas recent theories try to explain why a particular playful response was emitted.

The Nature of Theory

Before moving to the critical analyses of the various theories of play, some insight into the nature and role of theory in behavioral science and practice is necessary.

The world is a blooming buzzing confusion of events. We categorize and systematize; arrange the events by causes and effects, and by so doing simplify the world; bring order to its confusion. Man struggles constantly to reduce the bewildering array of events to some simpler and unified explanation. He theorizes.

> A theory is a set of interrelated constructs (concepts), definitions, and propositions that present a systematic view of the phenomena by specifying relations among variables with the purpose of explaining and predicting [Kerlinger, 1967, p. 11].

The preceding definition clearly applies to complex explanations like those of Lewin in *Field Theory in Social Science* (1951) or Hull in *Principles of Behavior* (1943). These theories were extensive, explicitly stated, and dealt with a vast area of human behavior.

In comparison, the extant "theories" of play are really explanatory ideas or concepts that are neither explicit nor extensive enough to be properly classified as theories. Most have been elevated by common parlance to the rank of theory. However, to avoid confusion they will be referred to as theories, although they are only the central idea around which, perhaps, theories could have been built.

Theories by Kerlinger's definition are two-edged; they explain events that have occurred and predict which events are likely to occur. Their value is determined by the success with which they do this.

The phenomenon, play, is a bewildering variety of behaviors emitted under circumstances in which many concepts of behavior suggest that the organism should be quiescent. The difficulty of defining it objectively and explaining its causes and effects has intrigued mankind for centuries. Our need for a rational system to explain play has led to a variety of theories. Because these theories influence the thinking about play and the planning and programming that is undertaken as a result, they require critical evaluation.

The problem with theorizing is knowing when to stop. For example, at the simplest level in behavioral science, an explanation for behavior can stop with a satisfactorily predictive statement that links events or contingencies in the environment with ensuing behavior. Thus, for any individual it is possible to chart the effect of a variety of contingencies on various behaviors. When this is done, it is then possible to alter the probability of various behaviors being emitted. Thus, a hungry rat will tend to increase the emission of responses that have in the past led to food. In the same way a child will tend to do things that lead to positive reinforcement or avoidance of aversive stimuli. This has proved to be a powerful method of thinking about and controlling behavior, and very useful in clinical practice since it takes into account individual differences. However, it requires careful analysis of the relationship between particular contingencies and the responding of a particular child. This is the essential ingredient in the technology for manipulating behavior called behavior modification.

While behavior modification establishes and exploits what works for any individual, it is derived, at the simplest level of abstraction, from the concept that some events are rewarding, and that an animal or child will tend to emit the responses for which rewards are contingent. There are obvious patterns extending over children so that it is worthwhile to try to formulate generalizations about classes of events that are likely to be rewarding. At this point the connections are abstracted or induced.

Asking the question "What is the causal connection between response and contingency?" leads to the next level of abstraction in dealing with the problem. At this point the mechanisms, be they physiological or psychological, are suggested whereby the lack of some attribute in the internal environment increases in aversiveness with deprivation. In some instances the reward for the organism may be the relief from aversive stimuli generated by the mechanism sensing the lack. In others the reward may be the generation of stimuli that are positively reinforcing or pleasant. This kind of explanation appears to attack the causal link between the state of environment or the organism and its responses, but

on reduction it is really no more than a sophisticated way of saying that some stimuli encourage and others discourage behavior. However, regions in the brain have been identified which produce positive or negative effects on behavior. Animals with chronic implants into the brain can be punished or rewarded by tiny electric currents according to the placement of the electrode.

It is possible to escalate the sophistication of a causal explanation to the point where answers are attempted for questions about exactly how a particular sensing mechanism signals the lack and reinforces the provision of the needed materials or stimuli, etc. Since theory is concerned with useful explanation of the relationships between phenomena, there comes a point for some workers when increasingly complex and fine-grained analyses of the causal mechanisms cease to produce improvements in the control of the phenomenon.

Theories are valuable to the extent that they are confirmable or testable (Popper, 1961). They must allow for statements that are predictive. Theories that cannot lead to testable predictions cannot be tested and rejected, but then neither can they improve control over the phenomena they seek to explain.

Concepts of the confirmability of a theory have become more elastic over time as the philosophy of pragmatism has become more powerful. Theories were originally held to be confirmed only if they were verifiable beyond doubt. Thus, a confirmed theory in these terms coincided with a notion like absolute truth. Next, theories were acceptable until they were conclusively disproved—they were innocent (or true) till proven guilty. Later yet, theories could make probability statements about outcomes, meaning that some proportion of the time they predicted outcomes. The willingness of the user to accept different levels of reliability determined a theory's acceptance. Now, theory is held only relatively confirmable, capable of neither conclusive proof nor rejection, and has been relegated to the position of a conceptual tool, its value determined by its usefulness. Usefulness is defined as capacity to explain data and predict outcomes.

From a practical viewpoint theories linking phenomena are valuable if the mechanisms postulated as the cause are manipulable by those interested in controlling the subsequent events. They are useful to the extent that they convey an advantage to those understanding and using them.

For those concerned with the management of play behavior, it is only worthwhile developing increasingly sophisticated theories to explain the behavior to the extent that it is possible to manipulate the postulated mechanisms. Thus, there is little point in developing theories in this context that would depend on chronically implanted electrodes in the brain. However, the various theories explaining play must be held in the balance and evaluated in the light of the existing data and body of knowledge concerning play.

Surplus Energy Theories of Play

The idea that surplus energy is the motive for play has proved attractive to many concerned with play. The essence of the idea has appeared in many formulations, and Groos (1898) analyzes the history of the idea and traces its development from the poet Schiller in 1800 to its formal appearance in Spencer's writings in 1855 (1896). Schiller's original idea, taken up by Spencer and formalized, was that "The animal works when some want is the motive for his activity, and plays when the superabundance of energy forms this motive—when overflowing life itself urges him to action [Groos, 1898, p. 2]." The idea that the organism played in order to expend a surplus of energy accumulated by virtue of not having had to expend that on the work of survival was obviously a common one during the early nineteenth century since Groos cites other authors who express the same idea.

This theory is commonly held to rest on the notion that an organism is capable of generating a finite level of energy that *must* be expended. The energy is available to the animal for expenditure on the struggle for survival. To the extent that the animal successfully and efficiently meets the challenges of its environment with the expenditure of less energy than is available, a surplus results. The surplus is seen to accumulate and eventually induces its expenditure on nonproductive activity or play. This concept explains the higher frequency of play behavior in young animals in terms of their lighter burden of survival activities. The more adults carry the load in the struggle for survival or the work of continuing existence, the more energy is available for play in the young who are not carrying that load (see Table 3.1, pp. 46–47).

The surplus energy motive for play was reiterated by Tolman in 1932. Tolman postulated a sensory-motor-hunger to account for behavior left over after satisfaction of the food-, sex-, contact-, and rest-hungers. The sensory-motor-hunger, which was also called aesthetic or play hunger, Tolman described as a need ". . . to get 'mild and harmonious' fatigues of their discriminative, manipulative and means end 'faculties' . . ."

> . . . We assume, in short, that when, in the course of general metabolism, one of the higher organisms is in a relatively natural state of metabolic condition, i.e., in a condition in which none of his other appetites or aversions is strongly engaged, that such an organism is apt to be in a condition

of unspent energy. And such a condition, we shall assume, is in itself a state of physiological disequilibrium which requires a complementary fatigue for neutralization and quiescence [Tolman, 1967, pp. 278–292].

This concept has serious shortcomings, many examples of which will spring to mind. First, it is quite obvious the animals will play until the energy supply systems have not only expended any surplus but have incurred considerable debt. Looking at this another way, animals will emit play behavior even though apparently fatigued. To take an example from common experience, remember an occasion when a child or dog returns from, say, a long walk. They both walk wearily, behaving in a way which communicates that they are all but exhausted. However, on arrival, if some new and arousing opportunity is presented, the fatigue is forgotten. It seems that animals play at some considerable cost, not just to expend a surplus.

A further objection can be raised based on what Spencer called the Doctrine of Evolution. In general, the doctrine states that attributes persist and are exaggerated by selection if they convey some advantage, and the corollary is simply that the possessor of a disadvantageous attribute tends to be selected against.

The principle of selection by the pressures of the environment would logically, over time, have tailored the energy level of each species to requirements of its environmental niche. It can be argued, then, that the surplus energy, which forces the animal to expend energy in nonproductive interactions with the environment, increases the exposure of the animal to the dangers inherent in the environment. The play of young animals, to the extent that it takes them outside the den, attracts attention, and relaxes their vigilance, would seem to be a negative attribute. Thus, those animals with more appropriate energy levels should be selected. However, the continued existence of play over time and the increase in the quantity of play with increasing complexity of animals indicate that the proclivity to play conveys a selective advantage at best, or at worst is selectively neutral.

On another front, it is frequently argued that the theory does explain the behavior of children and animals who have experienced enforced quiescence or response deprivation and who emit gross muscular, diffuse, and vigorous activity on release. In such cases the quantity of energy expended should increase with increased response deprivation. This argument could presumably be carried to the point where the energy surplus was so great that no stimuli would be needed to trigger its expenditure, and behavior would be emitted spontaneously. The stereotyped behavior of animals and children kept under conditions of response deprivation, which pose serious problems for those managing mentally ill and retarded children and zoo animals (Morris, 1962; Hediger, 1950), can perhaps be explained in this way. Stereotyped responses are "frequent, almost mechanical repetition of a posture or movement which varies only slightly in form from time to time, and which serves no obvious functions [Davenport & Menzel, 1963, p. 99]." Their function might well be merely to expend energy.

These conceptions of the theory, however, would be best served if the spenders of the surplus energy spent it in ways that most efficiently eliminated the surplus. However, neither the stereotyped responses, nor the diffuse activity emitted in response to stimuli in the environment that are apparently brought about by response deprivation necessarily use the large muscle masses. Stereotyped responses may range from quite vigorous rocking movements, small manipulative responses, to the slow massive "figure of eight" walking patterns of caged animals (Hediger, 1950). It may be that the stereotypies act as a behavioral safety valve, blowing off energy at the rate at which it accumulates. In this case relatively small rates of expenditure are sufficient to prevent the accumulation of an intolerable surplus.

The diffuse but intense activity emitted by children after deprivation is short-lived. Personal observation indicates the brief explosion of running and shouting is followed by extended playful activity of lesser intensity. If the surplus is eliminated by the initial brief spurt, then why do the children continue their other activities? If the spurt does not eliminate the surplus, why do the children reduce the rate of elimination of the surplus? It is possible to conceive of homeostatic explanations that postulate an initial burst of intense activity, but these do not satisfactorily salvage the theory from the initial major objections.

This is not to say that fatigue or other stress (Selye, 1956) does not influence the quantity of energy expended on play. The tired or sick animal will play less vigorously, and perhaps spasmodically, but it will play. A healthy rested animal, other things being equal, will play more, but surplus energy is not necessary for play.

Over the years much of the original insight into the causes of play that Spencer had has been lost. He is not usually given credit for an idea that has resurfaced recently, and he is labelled falsely as the originator of the simplistic surplus energy theory. He should be remembered by play theorists for the following quotation:

> Every one of the mental powers, then, being subject to this law, that its organ when dormant for an interval longer than ordinary becomes unusually ready to act, unusually ready to have its correlative feelings aroused, giving an unusual readiness to enter upon all the correlative activities; it happens that a stimulation of these activities is easily fallen into, where

circumstances offer it in place of the real activities. Hence play of all kinds—hence this tendency to superfluous and useless exercise of faculties that have been quiescent [Spencer, 1896, pp. 629–630].

This quotation merely claims that the response threshold is diminished by inactivity and is not the same formulation of the surplus energy theory of play that has been handed down to us by tradition (see Groos, 1898, pp. 4–5).

The concept of increased excitability as a result of deprivation is a basic one in motivational psychology. The deprivation of opportunity to respond lowers the threshold at which a behavior is elicited by relevant stimuli. After deprivation, less intense stimulation is necessary to elicit a response, or, as a corollary, the original stimuli elicit stronger, longer, or faster responding. This idea postulates a different mechanism and seems capable of explaining more behavior than the surplus energy theory.

The surplus energy model implies that after enforced quiescence the expenditure of energy is rewarding, it becomes a motive of itself. The reduced response threshold, or increased excitability hypothesis, suggests that after enforced quiescence the animal should show increased tendency to react to the available stimuli, not necessarily with the expenditure of much energy. Thus, the animal should emit the behavior reinforced by the new situation more vigorously; the animal reacts appropriately to the attributes of the new situation or its demand characteristics. For example, when children are released to a playground after response deprivation they emit strongly the behavior demanded of them by the available stimuli. It remains to be seen what would happen if they were released to a quiet room, a library, or a movie theater, but the hypothesis would not suggest that they emit vigorous activity to expend energy.

At this point it is worth noting two ideas advanced by Groos that foreshadowed modern play theories and for which he is not customarily given credit. In the preface to his book *Play in Animals* (Groos, 1898), he formulated ideas that only now are seen as important because more recently propounded theories have allowed us to recognize them. He perceptively formulated quite directly in his writings in 1895 a concept that was labelled competence motivation (White, 1959) many years later. Groos saw that a major element in the motivation of play is, as he puts it, "joy in being a cause." This idea appears several times in his writings and although the methods of explanation are different from those of White, they contain the same basic notion.

Hidden in Groos's writing is a further idea that emerged much later as a theoretical concept of some importance. He cited Souriau who said, "When we indulge in exercise that requires the expenditure of much energy all our functions are quickened, the heart beats more rapidly, respiration is increased in frequency and in depth, and we experience a feeling of general well-being." "We are more alive and glad that we are [1898, pp. 289, 290]." Groos goes on to add "Besides these external effects of pleasurable feelings they are accompanied internally by a heightened excitation of the sensory and motor centers of the cerebrum, much like that produced by concentrated attention—a fact which points to the probable explanation of the physiological side of pleasure [1898, p. 289]." This is an almost uncanny precursor of present-day thinking concerning arousal and attention and its mediation by the reticulate arousal system in the brain. So once again Groos appears to have conceptually scooped later thinkers. In addition to his early debunking of surplus energy theories, Groos presented two ideas of motivation that were to appear much later, namely, competence motivation and arousal mechanisms.

However, Beach (1945) finally scotches the idea that play is caused by surplus energy by demonstrating that the notion is circular.

> Suggestions of this sort have little to recommend them. In the first place they are based upon the most obvious sort of circular reasoning. The catch lies in the definition of the term "surplus." When a cat chases, catches and devours a mouse, a certain amount of energy is expended; but no one suggests that this is extra, or surplus energy. Now, when the same cat chases, catches and chews on a rubber ball, an equal energy loss may occur; but in this case it is said to be surplus energy which has been released. Catching and eating mice is serious business for the cat (or at least the human observer thinks that it *should be*); whereas pursuit of a rubber ball serves no obvious, immediate and practical end (insofar as the observer can tell). Therefore, ball chasing must be play, whereas mouse chasing is not play. Refraining for the moment from commenting upon the anthropomorphic reasoning involved, we can see that the decision as to whether or not the expended energy is surplus energy, depends upon the interpretation of the behavior as playful or serious. Therefore, to set up as one criterion or explanation of play the condition that it involves the release of surplus energy is to do no more than complete the circle [Beach, 1945, pp. 527–528].

This notion of the circularity of defining play in terms of the observer's imputed motive was also raised by Schlosberg (1947) and underlies a major difficulty in thinking and theorizing on play.

Some research has accumulated that bears on the problem of surplus energy. The animal work shows, for example, that rats will work for an opportunity to run in an exercise wheel or through a maze. Some work also shows that deprivation of opportunities to be active produces some elevation of activity on release from deprivation. The model presumes these animals are driven by a need to be active and the hydraulic model would predict that energy would accumulate and eventually generate an explosive compensatory burst of activity on presentation of opportunities to be active.

Lore (1968) reviewed the work that bears on this concept of an activity drive. As usual the results were complex. Some deprivations reduced activity, and some extended deprivations disorganized the animals so that they emitted stereotyped responses even when they were not deprived. The varying definitions of activity and the varying conditions of deprivation prevented any clear-cut consensus on the effects of response deprivation. Lore concluded that there was "remarkably little evidence that would justify the postulation of an autonomous activity drive [1968, p. 569]."

Some recent work with children suggests that the mere burning of energy does not explain their behavior. Children exhibiting restlessness, distractibility, and emotional lability are often labelled hyperactive and hyperactivity is a most common diagnosis attached to mentally retarded and emotionally disturbed children. According to adults who work with these children, they have too much energy to allow them to meet the constraints of various social and school settings by inhibiting their activity levels. These children therefore presumably possess a superabundance of energy to be consumed. The surplus energy theory should hold strongly for them. However, the early data investigating the total activity levels of these children suggests that they do not exceed the normal ranges of energy expended during a day (Schulman, Kaspar & Throne, 1965). The energy hypothesis that remains is that these children have a small capacity for a surplus. They cannot tolerate for long deviations from their idiosyncratic energy expenditure levels. Social constraints on their activity cause their surplus to build.

Other research on the play of children (Wade, Ellis & Bohrer, 1971) shows that the activity of children is periodic. In a free-range, children were shown to oscillate complexly between levels of high and low activity with frequencies of 15 minutes' duration superimposed on a larger cycle of 40 minutes. An explanation in terms of surplus energy theory would be that the children were oscillating between periods of rest when a surplus would build and periods of activity when the surplus would be squandered. However, in this experiment the authors were able to manipulate the periodicity by varying the complexity of the play setting. Increasing complexity was achieved by increasing the number of others playing and the amount of play equipment. The quantity of apparatus did not influence this behavior but the number of playmates did.

For two reasons the data do not support the concept of surplus energy being the motive for the play that took place. First, the patterns of expenditure fell to some extent under the control of experimenters. Had the system governing the play behavior been intrinsic to the children, the generation of surplus energy would have continued independently. Second, the children's initial activity level on being placed in the setting was high.

The play sessions started at a peak, even though the children had not been deprived of opportunities to respond beforehand. An explanation more convincing than the presence of surplus energy is that the children were immediately aroused to activity by the stimulating properties of the play setting. The best explanation may be that the alternation between relatively high levels of energy expenditure was created by the need to reduce the high levels of activity regularly to restore the homeostatic balance. In a sense, then, the troughs were caused by the opposite of a surplus; the subjects may have incurred energy debts and reduced their activity level while they repaid them.

Energy as a physical concept with hydraulic properties does not satisfactorily explain play (Hinde, 1960). Although energy is necessary for play in that fatigue and ill-health reduces the supply, it does not explain the phenomenon.

Play as Relaxation

Sustained responding of any kind seems to build up an aversion to its continuation. Various ideas exist as to where and what builds up to reduce the tendency for further like responding, but the notion corresponds to the layman's view of fatigue. If sleep is not required, then the organism needs to emit other responses that allow the fatigued elements to regenerate. This basic concept supports two closely related theories of play—the recreation theory and the more recent relaxation theory of Patrick (1916).

Sapora and Mitchell cite Lazarus as saying, "After work we require rest which accomplishes recuperation. But hardly ever does mere empty, inactive rest suffice for recuperation [Sapora & Mitchell, 1961, p. 81]." Lazarus advises that frequently the noxious byproducts of sustained responding are best eliminated by active play. However, this does not specify which activities, apart from sleep, will work. Patrick (1916) went further and had clear ideas as to which activities were best.

Patrick saw the role of play and sports as restorative; a necessary recuperation from work. His explanation of why some activities were restorative and others were not, follows:

> There is a striking similarity between the plays of children and the sports of men on the one hand and the pursuits of primitive man on the other.

> This similarity is due to the fact that those mental powers upon which advancing civilization depends, especially voluntary and sustained attention, concentration, analysis and abstraction, are undeveloped in the child and subject to rapid fatigue in the adult. Hence, the child's activities and the play activities of the adult tend always to take the form of old racial pursuits [Patrick, 1916, pp. 48–49].

Lazarus seems to have been the wiser theorist, apparently inciting us merely to change activities with the onset of fatigue. Patrick, by specifying those ancient phyletic activities that our species had become well adapted to over the aeons of our evolution, opened himself to all the criticisms of the recapitulation theory of play. Also, he failed to answer why those engaged in the racially ancient motor responses of physical labor still seem to seek for play and recreative activity. To the extent that manual workers do not indulge in "voluntary sustained attention, concentration, analysis and abstraction" they should need less restoration by playful activity. This notion stands up to examination only insofar as it explains the play and recreation activities of a subset of adults involved in mental rather than physical labor.

However, without doubt much of the work of the modern world, both mental and physical, meets Patrick's definition of work. "Work . . . will include all those activities in which by means of sustained voluntary attention one holds one's self down to a given task for the sake of some end to be attained other than the activity itself [Patrick, 1916, pp. 47–48]." Lazarus' concept presumably holds that any activity that contrasts with the characteristics of a person's work is suitable for his restoration, Patrick went too far by restricting playful activity to racially ancient behavior and had to limit his case to a certain type of work.

In explaining play in children, Patrick's concepts also run aground. If play is motivated by the need to recuperate from work, then why do children (or other nonworkers) play? Patrick's view of the child and his play is that a child is active because he is a child; that since the child is not productive or engaged in work, then his activity is play.

> The child does not play because of surplus energy, for under normal conditions all his energy is expended in play; the child is playing animal. Nor does he play because of an instinctive need of practice and preparation for life's serious duties, for the form of the latter is constantly changing, while the play of children remains much the same from year to year and century to century. Nor finally does he play because it is necessary for his complete growth that he should pass through several stages of racial history. He plays because he is a child and to the child's natural and active life we give the name "play" to distinguish it from the life of conscious self-direction, of strain, and effort and inhibition which evoluton has imposed on the adult human being [Patrick, 1916, pp. 79–80].

In addition to his difficulty in categorizing a child's playful activity as something apart from conscious self-direction, strain, and effort, Patrick has no explanation for the play behavior of children other than that it is *natural* and instinctive.

Relaxation and Surplus Energy Theory Reconciled

The two opposing views of play as the expression of surplus energy on the one hand and as restitution of energies on the other, are reconcilable. Reconciliation depends on rejecting the notion that there is one generalized energy source, and one central location of fatigue. It is possible to consider that the sustained use of one set of responses tires only those parts involved and that the resources of parts not concerned with the response are therefore not tapped. Thus, while one part works and becomes fatigued, other parts acquire increased potential for responding. Groos in his second book, published originally in 1898, deals with just this point.

> There are two leading principles which must ground a physiological theory of play—namely the discharge of surplus energy and recreation for exhausted powers. They may operate simultaneously since acts supplying recreation to exhausted forces may at the same time call into play other powers and thus afford the needed discharge for them. In many cases, and especially in youth, the first principles seem to act alone, while on the other hand play may be solely recreation, without any dependence on a store of surplus energy [Groos, 1901, p. 368].

These two views comprise a simplistic view of behavior as motivated by too much energy, or its opposite, too much fatigue. Their opposite predictions are avoided by allowing their complementary effects to cancel out within the individual. But the systems depend too much on the physical concept of energy (Hinde, 1960) that can be stored and transformed. Each model can be attacked separately. However, to destroy the concepts inherent in their interaction is more difficult. If "surplus energy" is redefined as an increased tendency to respond in a response system after a period in which there have been no responses emitted and that fatigue is the opposite, then each response system which can store energy and become fatigued is unstable. The system will oscillate between activity and rest as first one phase, then the other is satisfied.

In any individual there are many response systems, all of which should alternate between the need to be exercised and to recuperate. Since a limited number of responses can be emitted at the same time there should be a continual interplay as the various response systems compete and respond for the opportunity to expend their surpluses. While each system is quiescent it will be accumulating a surplus, and the pressure for it to be expended will increase. Presumably the most pressing needs will be served first. However, according to the strength of the tendency to respond, each response system will eventually achieve priority. The individual should eventually run the gamut of his response systems, as their respective surpluses are eliminated.

Groos's reconciliation of these two, apparently opposite, views of play leads to serious difficulties. It does not differentiate between a structural system and the myriad responses in which each one is implicated. Does the model address, say, the arm flexor or the available responses involving arm flexions? It does not predict which responses take priority, and does not explain why some responses are never emitted. The argument can best be considered a neat conceptual manipulation that handled two opposing ideas, but can be rejected at this time as a useful model for predicting why people play, in what way, and when.

Play as an Instinct

A major explanation for the enigma of play derived from early instinct theories of behavior. Instincts were seen to be innate or preexistent tendencies to emit the behavior in question: James saw them as ". . . the faculty of acting in such a way to produce certain ends, without foresight of the ends, and without previous education in the performance [1890, p. 383]." He added that "they are the functional correlatives of structure. With the presence of a certain organ goes, one may say, almost always a native aptitude for its use [James, 1890, p. 383]."

> Instincts have had a long history in scientific thinking. The instinct concept can be traced from early philosophies which set man apart from the rest of the living world and sought for him some divine affinity. This was achieved by claiming for man alone the power of reason. By a process of elimination the behavior of animals was ascribed to their natural instincts [Beach, 1966, p. 9].

Later, however, it was accepted that man possessed instincts and that they were a convenient way to explain behavior. Often the instinct was named by the observer's perception of the purpose served by the behavior observed. For example, a response that served the survival of the animal was presumed to be motivated by an instinct for self-preservation.

James's concept of an instinct was that it was not an invariant tendency to respond. Rather instincts were subject to competition for dominance and control of the organism from all the other tendencies, both innate and acquired   Thus, whether a particular instinct gave rise to behavior

CLASSICAL THEORIES OF PLAY   37

was determined by the interaction of all the impulses to action and in-
action.   The more complex the animal, the less likely the responses will
be simply reflexive.

James felt that man had more instincts and reasoning capacity than
all other animals and so man "loses the 'instinctive' demeanor and appears to lead a life of hesitation and choice, an intellectual life; not, however, because he has no instincts—rather because he has so many that
they block each other's path [1890, p. 383]." Instincts were the early psychologists' solution to the theoretical questions concerning the motive
for behavior and how behavior common to a species was communicated.

A common theory of play which emanates from these times is that play
is caused by instinctive need to play.   McDougall (1923) is commonly held
responsible for the formulating of this concept.   McDougall listed a number of primary instincts:

> Fear with its impulse to flee
> Disgust
> Curiosity
> Anger
> Self-assertion
> Submission
> Parental instinct
> Reproduction
> Hunger
> Gregariousness
> Collection
> Construction

and then added a group of minor tendencies among which was one to
play.   Spencer (1896, Vol. 1, p. 433), Woodworth (1921), and James
(1890), all discussed instinct as an important source of motivation for
the behavior they observed.   However, again one author, McDougall,
has been traditionally assigned credit for an idea that was deeply-embed-
ded in the thinking of the time.

Despite the traditional view of McDougall as the originator of the instinct theory of play he did not advance the idea that there was a specific
instinct motivating play.   In fact, in 1923 he argued against there being
a specific play instinct.

> It is clear that in play all (almost all) of the motor mechanisms possessed
> by the creature may be brought into action. . . . if an instinct were
> merely a motor mechanism, play would have to be regarded as an expres-
> sion of not one instinct but of many, or of all [McDougall, 1923, p. 170].

He added a rider to this comment that specified when the animal would emit play responses.

> Since then, neither the occasions, nor the symptoms, nor the movements of the playing animals, are those characteristic of the instinctive activities which play simulates, we are driven to the conclusion that the corresponding instincts are not really at work (or at play). I suggest that animals are merely exercising their various motor mechanisms in turn under the guidance of their sense organs, and finding pleasure or satisfaction in so doing. Play is activity for its own sake, or, more probably, it is the purposeless activity, striving toward no goal. Whence, then, comes the energy that sustains it? The answer is that I think that the well fed and well rested animal, especially the young animal, has a surplus of nervous energy which works through the channels of the various motor mechanisms. We see this in the caged beast which prowls round and round, or from side to side. . . . we see it in the school boys, who, after growing more and more fidgety, spring out into the playground, running and shouting and laughing aimlessly and independently of any exciting objects [McDougall, 1923, p. 171].

Thus, McDougall was still subject to the notions of the surplus energy theories of behavior. His "tendency for play" was merely surplus energy spilling over and inciting a multitude of purposeless responses, usually called forth by specific instincts.

The fall of instinct started when behaviorists began to question the necessary innate or inherited nature of the motives for apparently unlearned responses. Doubts were raised whether the apparently inherited behavior had not been acquired before birth or hatching, or whether it had been created by the experiences of the parent, etc. While the argument raged at the substantive level as to whether this or that behavior was acquired or innate, the concept of instinct came to be seen as a less helpful construct.

Although James called an instinct a compound reflex-action (1890, p. 432), it is quite obvious that what are classified as instincts in McDougall's terms are large abstractions or categorizations of what must be multitudes of organized compound reflex-actions. Thus, there was a tendency to continually elaborate on the lists of instincts to account for more behavior. This did not dismay James. He felt that it was possible for each of the myriad different responses emitted by a complex organism to be called forth by inherited mechanisms or instincts.

> At first this view astounds us by the enormous number of special adjustments it supposes animals to possess ready made in anticipation of the outer things among which they dwell. Can mutual dependence be so

intricate and go so far? Is each thing born fitted to particular other things, and to them exclusively, as locks are fitted to their keys? Undoubtedly this must be believed to be so [James, 1890, p. 384].

The inherent illogic of this view was pointed out by Bernard in 1926. He claimed that all the instinct psychologists were doing was formulating an instinct for each class of behavior they wished to explain. Thus, if the observer could perceive a group of behaviors that had apparently some common attribute, he could formulate a new instinct. For example, if the change of position of the organism is taken as a category using this system, then crawling, rolling, walking, running, etc., in a child would be explained in terms of an instinct for locomotion.

> An instinct is a biological fact and it is a unit character, or it does not exist. It is structural. It is not possible to inherit an abstraction. The activity, which ordinarily by a species of metonymy is miscalled the instinct, is of course not inherited. The actual instinct which is inherited is the unit organization of the neurons, the physiological and neurological bases of which lie back of and give form to the activity or resulting behavior. The behavior is the visible manifestation of the structural neural organization. The behavior is the response of this neural-muscular organization of the organism to environmental pressures. Only the structural organization can be inherited and therefore be an instinct. A true classification of the instincts would be a description of these various neural mechanisms [Bernard, 1926, p. 17].

Instinct theories are prime targets for an absurd reduction to the statement that since a response was emitted, it must have been caused by its instinct. The way out of the polemic concerning unlearned and learned behavior was suggested by Beach.

> To remedy the present confused situation it is necessary first to refrain from premature classification of those kinds of behavior that are currently defined as unlearned. Until they have been systematically analyzed, it will remain impossible to decide whether these numerous response patterns belong in one or a dozen different categories.
>
> The analysis that is needed involves two types of approach. One rests upon determination of the relationships existing between genes and behavior. The other consists of studying the development of various behavior patterns in the individual, and determining the number and kinds of factors that normally control the final form of the response.
>
> When these methods have been applied to the various types of behavior which today are called "instinctive," the concept of instinct will disappear, to be replaced by scientifically valid and useful explanations [Beach, 1966, p. 16].

The application of Beach's recommendations to play behavior would result in two kinds of analyses. One would deal with characteristics that persist across generations between and within species that determine in a given environment the nature of playful behavior, an example being the concepts of neophilia and neophobia advanced by Morris (1962, 1964). The other approach would be to study the way in which play behavior varies in accordance with variations in the environment over time; to establish the causal links that exist between antecedent events in the environment and emitted behavior. While both areas are available for the study in man, in practice, only environmental manipulations are currently available for the modification of play or other behavior since we cannot manipulate the genetic make-up of an individual.

Play as Preparation

Although, in general, instinct and instinct theories of play have fallen into disrepute, a derivative of the early instinct theories still lingers. Play is still discussed as preparation for adult life, and this notion was forcefully presented by Groos in his book *The Play of Animals*.

Groos's concept of play as preparation descended from his view of adult behavior as instinctive. The instinct controlling any aspect of adult behavior, to be perfect, should appear complete at an appropriate time in the life-cycle of the animal. Since instincts are not inherited in their final and exact form, practice is needed to perfect them. Play, the prior exercise of behaviors imperfectly inherited, allows the animal to perfect his instinctive skills to the point that later, when they become critical, they will be effective.

> Finally, in estimating the biological significance of play at its true worth, the thought was suggested that perhaps the very existence of youth is largely for the sake of play.
>
> Animals do not play because they are young but they have their youth because they must play [Groos, 1898, p. 76]. . . . for only by so doing can they supplement the insufficient hereditary endowment with individual experience in view of the coming tasks of life [Groos, 1898, p. 75].

There are problems with postulating play as preparation for adult life. First, the acts practiced are not serious; they are carried on in a situation where the harsh contingencies of the real world are suspended. Mistakes are not accompanied by deleterious reactions, and in fact may not be accompanied by attention to the end products of the behavior. If the players are truly attentive to the processes themselves and ignore the final result, then learning should be nonexistent since there will have been no feedback to positively reinforce some aspects of the behavior and the process will extinguish the inappropriate elements. It is unrealistic to claim that the end products of play behavior will go unnoticed by the players, and so some selective reinforcement will take place, but the rate of acquisition of the appropriate adult responses, the purpose of play, will be slowed.

The major difficulty with this theory stems from the necessity of imputing into the play behavior some preexisting knowledge of which responses will be needed during the serious times ahead. How does each organism know which response will be needed? This prescience requires exactly the same kind of exact knowledge to be inherited as was avoided by allowing instincts to be imperfect general tendencies.

The very animals that play most are those animals which exhibit variable and adaptive behavior as adults and tend to inhabit environmental niches where conditions are not fixed. Patterns of behavior fixed by some preexistent process would not work to the advantage of the entrepreneurs of the animal kingdom.

Groos had to add another ingredient to this picture to have play result in improvements in performance: an instinct for imitation.

> By means of imitation animals learn perfectly those things for which they have imperfect hereditary predispositions.
> We then reach the following conclusion in our play inquiry—namely, that all youthful play is founded on instinct. These instincts are not so stamped in all their details on the brain as they would have to be if the first expressions were to be in serious acts. Therefore, they appear in youth, and must be perfected during that period by constant practice [Groos, 1898, p. 79].

The young animal copies in his play the serious activities of the surrounding adults. Since fit animals tend to survive, the use of existing adults as models will tend to produce practice of appropriate responses, and hence fit the young imitators to their adult role.

This procedure would allow for the ready transmission of behaviors already extant in the group, and imitation clearly occupies a major part of the play of the young. However, the explanation does not yet bridge the gap from the history of the individual to the unknown challenges of the future. Only to the extent that the young imitate the problem-solving behavior exhibited by others and thereby improve their capacity to solve problems can imitative behavior be said to be preparatory. Acquiring a specific skill is not necessarily preparatory, but learning how to achieve specific skills is.

Groos made a basic teleological error in assuming that because play existed, it existed in order to prepare the adult. Adults who have played appropriately may be more successful in meeting the selective pressures of the environment, but to claim that play exists as preparation reverses the process, and is unacceptable.

Much of the contemporary concern for providing meaningful play experiences for our young stems from a desire to realize the potentials of the child, at the individual level, and thereby collectively nurturing our human resources. However, the mistake made by Groos is not inherent in these efforts. The concern for improving our young lies in the adult, not in the children themselves. They play without a concern for the future payoff their experiences may bring.

Play as Recapitulation

The theory of play as recapitulation argues that the process of development of an organism recapitulates the history of its development as a species. This idea stems from a Darwinian conception of evolution where there exists a clear line in development of the characteristics of the species. The continuous process of modification that gave rise to a species is rapidly summarized and recapitulated in the form and behavior of the young of a species. Embryologically this makes some sense since the tiny embryo, as it increases in complexity, follows some of the same stages that seem to have been followed in our evolution to the present. For example, at one point the human embryo possesses rudimentary gill arches that are homologous to the developing arches in a fish embryo. They are later incorporated into a variety of structures in the head and neck. The embryo of a mammal seems to pass through stages of increasing complexity that bear some similarity to the taxonomic structure of the phyla of the animal kingdom. Ontogeny, in a limited sense, seems to recapitulate morphologic phylogeny during the early stages of life. This theory extends that concept to explanations of behavior. The behavior of the young animal was seen to mirror the behavioral evolution of the species. To emerge, this idea required a mixture of the ideas of evolution with instinct theories of behavior. Thus, an individual inherits instincts to emit behavior during its development that recapitulates the history of the phylum and species.

> It appears to be not only true that the body rehearses the life of the race; it appears to be true that the mind must do so also, and that the plays of children are the rehearsal of the activities of the race during forgotten ages —not necessarily the self-same activities, but activities involving the same bodily and mental qualities. Putting it exactly, play is the ontogenetic rehearsal of the phylogenetic series [Gulick, 1898 p. 803].

This theory emerged at the same time that Groos presented his theory that play was preparation, but advanced the opposite view. Objections to play as preparatory activity were voiced by Hall who advanced a similar view to Gulick.

> The view of Groos that play is practice for future adult activities is very partial, superficial and perverse. It ignores the past where lie the keys to all play activities. . . . In play every word and movement is instinct with heredity. Thus, we rehearse the activities of our ancestors, back we know not how far, and repeat their life's work in summative and adumbrated ways. . . . Thus, stage by stage we reenact their lives [Hall, 1916, pp. 202–203].

This theory of behavior when applied to play and games argues that playful responses emitted by the developing child incorporate the skills of past generations.

> Some of the elements (of play) speak with a small voice, raucous with age. The first spontaneous movements in infancy are hieroglyphs, for most of which we have as yet no good key. Many elements are so impacted and felted together that we cannot analyze them. Many are extinct and many perhaps made but once and only hint things we cannot apprehend. Later the rehearsals are fuller, and their significance more intelligible, and in boyhood and youth the correspondences are plain to all who have eyes to see [Hall, 1916, p. 206].

The attraction of this theory for the times is exemplified by Gulick (1902) who tried to explain the popularity of some playful activities and games by asserting that those which reenacted activities from the history of the race were intrinsically more rewarding than newer activities. The play and games played by children and adults were susceptible to being ordered in complexity and much was made of the examples that fitted the idea. For example, baseball was seen as a direct and satisfying descendant of the early hunting activities of primitive man.

> . . . great games have gradually grown during the development of our kind, from simple practice throwing at a mark to the most modern form of baseball. Let not the comparatively recent date of the formulated game in its present form blind our eyes to the fact that in all countries of the world among rational human beings, those games depending on hard straight throwing, rapid running, and accurate, hard hitting with a club are prominent. They tell of the early pre-human ancestral activity when life was dependent upon these abilities [Gulick, 1902, pp. 62–63].

A major objection must be the extrapolation from some morphological similarities among developing embryos to the assumption that similar assertions can be made about behavior. The assumptions that the behavior of man at play follows the critical activities at various stages in the development of the race lead to some awkward exceptions that ruin the simplicity of the idea.

First, it is usually assumed that the theory requires that during development play follows a linear progression of developmental stages recapitulating the history of the race. Although this idea was hinted at in Gulick's and Hall's writings, it was not made explicit, and since then the theory seems to have taken on this additional assumption. However, it is not possible to perceive an orderly and linear progression in play that recapitulates more than the occasional survival activities of prehistoric man. While our children (and adults) swing clubs and draw on walls, they do not chip flints, or dig with horns, etc. The theory held more water in the era around the turn of the century when the society tended to be unable to provide play objects that were not derived simply from naturally available materials.

If the progression assumption is not made, then all that is required is that during play, activities that were critical during our phylogeny should appear sometime. Many such activities do appear. However, a better explanation would be that although our response repertoire has enormously increased over time, the essential similarity between our current form and that of our precursors predicts that quite often similar responses will be made since we are still bounded by the same anatomic constraints. It is going too far to say that such a response is made because the survival of our precursors depended on such responses.

The theory fails to set a limit in the course of evolution beyond which the behavior does not recapitulate the activities of simpler species lower on the evolutionary tree. For example, it is possible to advance the argument, without adding to the theory as formulated, that we should play like the early primates, or their precursors, or even the early mammals. To define a point in the process of evolution beyond which this concept no longer applies will require additional theorizing.

Finally, the theory does not explain the intense interest of man in toys that utilize contemporary technology, such as slot cars, dirt bikes, chemistry sets, and talking dolls. Nor does it explain sports and games that are concerned with the competitive application of technology to improving control of the environment in such sports as sailing, car racing, and gliding.

The theory was a natural outgrowth of the time when on the one hand we were becoming aware of the descent of man. On the other, the urbanization, technical complexity, and affluence of the society had not advanced to the present level and placed constraints on the kinds of activities indulged in during leisure. The resources were limited and simple, and the morphology of man remained similar to that of prehistoric man. The interaction of the materials available for play and the common physique produced play activities that bore a close resemblance to the productive activities undertaken during a primitive stage in our racial history. We now have a better view of these processes.

Summary

Over the years, much has been written by many authors concerning the older theories of play. As this process has continued, each author borrowed from a recent predecessor and the original thinkings of people like Groos, Hall, and Spencer were simplified and solidified in such a way that it is possible to be led astray. The early authors displayed considerable insight into the problems of defining play and advanced their concepts cautiously, hedging them with many restrictions.

In the process of evolution each of the major early thinkers on play has been connected to one much simplified element of their theories that has lived on in a way that does their original concept some discredit. For example, Groos suggested that a surplus energy theory of play was of limited value, since it quite clearly was not a necessary condition for play. He recognized as early as 1895 the very objections to a surplus energy theory of play that we advance today. It is surprising that the surplus energy theory of play ever became established in this century since the theory is eminently testable.

A major explanation for the survival of early theories of play must rest on the extent to which they seem to explain the puzzling behavior. Each one of the older theories clearly has some merit in that it seems to explain, albeit curiously, some aspects of children's and animals' behavior. The play behavior of children does indeed seem to recapitulate, in a simplistic way, some of the behaviors that were presumably important to the race as it evolved towards its present state. Also, there does seem to be a mysterious capacity for the child to emit behavior that is unrelated to productive activities. It is reassuring to claim that there just happens to be an instinct for play. It is more comfortable to ignore the shortcomings of the explanation. In addition, quite clearly the activities of the child or animals at play practiced, removed from real dangers, responses that were used by the adult organism for productive activities. The surplus energy theory of play, although a weak attempt to explain play, certainly seemed to account for the explosion of young children and animals into diffuse play activity after a period of quiescence or deprivation and still makes good sense to those who watch their young leave an arithmetic class to visit the playground.

Table 3.1

Classical Theories of Play

NAME	PLAY IS CAUSED:	THIS EXPLANATION ASSUMES THAT:	IT CAN BE CRITICIZED BECAUSE:
1a. Surplus Energy: I	by the existence of energy surplus to the needs of survival	1. energy is produced at a constant rate 2. if stored, storage is limited 3. excess must be expended 4. its expenditure is made on overt behavior which is by definition play	1. children play when fatigued or to the point of fatigue, so a surplus is not necessary for play 2. the process of evolution should have tailored the energy available to the energy required
1b. Surplus Energy: II	by increased tendency to respond after a period of response deprivation	1. all response systems of the body have a tendency to respond 2. the response threshold is lowered by a period of disuse 3. after periods of disuse, eventually all available responses should reach a low enough threshold to be discharged either by some stimulus events or spontaneously.	1. some responses available to the persons are never used
2. Instinct	by the inheritance of unlearned capacities to emit playful acts	1. the determinants of our behavior are inherited in the same way that we inherit the genetic code which determines our structure 2. some of those determinants cause play	1. It ignored the obvious capacity of the person to learn new responses that we classify as play 2. the facile naming of an instinct for each class of observed behavior is to do no more than to say, "Because there is play, there must be a cause which we will call an Instinct."

Theory	Play is caused...	Assumptions	Problems
3. Preparation	by the efforts of the player to prepare for later life	1. play is emitted only by persons preparing for new ways of responding 2. the player is instinctively prepared for responses that will be critical later 3. the instincts governing this are inherited imperfectly and youth is the period during which these imperfectly inherited mechanisms are perfected	1. play occurs most frequently in animals that live in rapidly changing circumstances 2. it requires that the player inherit the capacity to predict which responses will be critical later. This requires the inheritance of information about the future 3. people do not stop playing as adults, when presumably they are acceptably prepared
4. Recapitulation	by the player recapitulating the history of the development of the species during its development	1. the critical behaviors occurring during the evolution of man are encoded for inheritance 2. a person emits some approximation to all these behaviors during his development 3. since these behaviors are currently irrelevant they are play 4. the stages in our evolution will be followed in the individual's development	1. there is no linear progression in our play development that seems to mirror the development of a species. At one point, late boyhood and adolescence, there may be similarity between sports and games and the components of hunting, chasing, fighting, etc., but before and after there seems little relation 2. it does not explain play activities dependent on our advanced technology
5. Relaxation	by the need for an individual to emit responses other than those used in work to allow recuperation	1. players work 2. play involves the emission of responses different from those of work 3. the emission of different responses eliminates the noxious byproducts of work	1. it does not explain the use in play of activities also used in work 2. it does not explain the play of children—unless they are clearly working some part of their day

To the extent that each theory either explained puzzling aspects of behavior, or removed any responsibility for thinking about or planning for play behavior, thereby rendering the holder of the theory conceptually more comfortable, so they have survived. To the extent the various play theories explain the enigma of play, and prove useful in letting those whose interests lie in planning for play to make better predictions, they can compete actively, and eventually supplant the less useful theories of play. However, this process can only take place if those basing their work on the tenets of a particular theory are critical of its assumptions on the one hand and its capacity to predict events in the real world on the other. The classical theories are not a very promising group of theories.

RECENT THEORIES
OF PLAY

Chapter 4

Gilmore's second category for theories of play is a historical one. Theories of play fall into this category if they were initiated essentially during the period after the turn of the century. These theories are concerned with the actual form of the play behavior and attempt to link the antecedent and subsequent events via causes and effects. They are in most cases the derivatives of explanatory thrusts that were not originally concerned with play.

Two of the recent theories rely on the concept that the determinant of people's play or leisure choices is the nature of their work. Thus, people who perform their work tasks well and are satisfied by them, will tend to behave similarly during their leisure time. Juxtaposed to that, people who are frustrated by their work activities are likely to choose other forms of behavior during their leisure. These two theories, task generalization and task compensation, are not in opposition since they specify different subsets of the population as their targets. One applies to those satisfied by work, the other to those who cannot realize their goals through work.

Somewhat related to the idea that play is compensatory are the cathartic and psychoanalytic explanations. They share the notion that play in some way allows the restoration of equanimity in the person after unpleasant experiences or tendencies. These two explanations advance the ideas that play reduces aggression and frustration, and stress and anxiety, respectively. These explanations, including generalization and compensation, look backward at the antecedent experiences, and see play as a strategy for erasing or working out the effects of those experiences.

During recent times two further explanations have been advanced. One infers that play comes about by virtue of the cognitive structure of the individual and the other derives from the capacity of individuals to learn to play according to the dictates of the culture in which they find themselves. The prime explanatory system utilizing the cognitive dynamics of the developing child was developed by Piaget, and his theories of play are treated here. The cognitivists are naturally concerned with people in general and see each of them passing through common phases during development. While the content of each individual's interactions may vary, the structure of their thinking is locked into a system of developmental phases. Individuals advance to the next stage as a result of their experiencing the content of their preceding phase.

The view of play as learned from the culture is a recent theory conceived on a grander scale than the other recent theories. It still deals with the relation between antecedent events and subsequent behaviors but concerns itself with the communalities of experience and behavior that set one culture apart from another. It depends on the assumption that play is learned, and that what is learned is imposed by the complex constraints of the ecosystem within which the learner is embedded. Viewing a culture means looking at common events and behaviors rather than individual contingencies and responses. However, play as culturally determined and play as learned behavioral events are aligned on a continuum differing only in the detail with which the events are analyzed.

Unlike the classical theories, all of these explanations are more deeply rooted in the experiences of the individual than in his inheritance and their assumptions and shortcomings are summarized in Table 4.1 (see pp. 78–79).

Task Generalization and Compensation

The two theories of task generalization and compensation have been applied in the main to the selection of leisure activity by those in the work force. They both attempt to predict which kinds of activities will be selected by workers in the light of the characteristics of their work.

Task generalization is claimed to stem directly from the psychological concept of response generalization. Here a stimulus tends to evoke responses that have been evoked by stimuli similar to it in the past. Although response generalization was originally formulated in the context of extremely simple responses, e.g., birds pecking at keys, eye blinks, etc. (Kimble, 1961), it has been applied to the far more complex leisure choices and activities of adult man. In essence the theory states that adults will choose for their leisure activities those that are similar to ones that satisfy them at work. The leisure choices are made to allow the worker greater opportunity to emit behaviors he has developed and found satisfying. This theory ignores the problem of causality in the sense that

a worker might choose a work setting that he knows will be satisfying by virtue of his leisure experiences. At heart the theory must depend on the personality of the subject and argues that people will select work and leisure experiences that satisfy their needs. However, the concept is useful in that, since most people work, it might be possible to make inferences concerning leisure choices from the characteristics of their work (Breer & Locke, pp. 15–18).

Compensation theory suggests that adults select their leisure activities to compensate for the tendency of the work situation to deny satisfaction of their psychic needs. Thus, a worker denied opportunity for privacy might seek solitary activities when given the choice. To be predictive the theory requires that needs of the individual be defined. The needs must then be compared with the satisfactions of the job to detect missing ingredients that contribute to the psychic adjustment of the individual. These residual needs should then be met by appropriate leisure activities.

The two theories are compatible, since workers find satisfactions and frustrations in work and might make varied leisure selections that represent either generalization or compensation. Only careful analysis of an individual and his work would reveal which was which.

These two notions about leisure have given rise to some data. Hagedorn and Labowitz (1968) used a group of people that reflected work specializations in large organizations and tested the theories' ability to predict the workers' leisure-time participation in community associations. They argued that certain behaviors, norms, and values which are instrumental for task achievement are rewarded and learned. The learned behaviors are more likely to be generalized if the given task is similar and the work situation is a major source of skilled behavior. This generalization concept predicts that different kinds of workers will participate differently in community associations. Those workers in managerial or professional jobs should participate in community associations far more than those not practicing leadership. This hypothesis was supported clearly. The leaders and professionals participated in, as opposed to joined, more community associations and the best predictors of participation were the occupational leadership role and education.

This same study also tested in a limited way whether a desired behavioral outlet not provided in one situation would be sought in another. It was assumed, for example, that there is a need for positive social interactions by the workers. In the kind of large organization studied some members worked in comparative isolation, seldom influencing the decisions of the enterprise and having limited formal and informal contact with fellow workers. The compensation hypothesis predicts that these workers will join and participate in more community associations, and the prediction was supported by the data.

The study went into more detail, but in general found the two hypotheses of interest supported particularly when the measure predicted was participation or involvement in the association rather than just joining. The study was essentially concerned with the need for social interaction and suggests many other similar studies of the interplay of work and leisure with the various other "needs" of individuals.

In contrast to the preceding study, which was concerned with long-term or chronic effects on behavior, Witt and Bishop (1970) confirmed in a general way that leisure behavior varies according to the immediate antecedent experiences. They tested five theories of leisure activity that depended on the need for relaxation, catharsis, compensation, task generalization, and expenditure of surplus energy. The subjects were asked to report the type of leisure activity they would feel like doing if they had just had one of a variety of experiences. The various descriptions of experiences were devised carefully and presumed to exemplify situations that led to one of the five "need" states associated with the theories. The situations and the leisure activities to be selected reflected the environmental and cultural situation of the respondents, junior college students.

The concept of compensation was not supported in this study. Both situations in the study that were designed to evince compensatory activity were descriptions of failure situations. The respondents did not wish to return to work-oriented nor to social or entertaining settings. They claimed they would withdraw from people or visit a friend. Also, the concept of task generalization was not supported. Respondents claimed that if they had worked hard and successfully they were inclined to take it easy rather than to choose work-oriented leisure activity. This study failed to elicit in the reported, rather than actual, choices of leisure activities, a tendency to generalize from or compensate for a specific antecedent experience suggested by the authors. The hypotheses about leisure choices as a result of antecedent experience that suggested catharsis, the expenditure of energy hypotheses, and restorative and diversionary relaxation tended to be supported. Hagedorn and Labowitz, in their study spanning ten months, showed that stable participation in community associations seems to be accounted for in part by generalization and compensation, whereas Witt and Bishop found no such tendency.

The contradictory trends in these two recent studies can be resolved by either dismissing the Witt and Bishop finding as an ineffective test, or looking closely at the nature of the comparison. Witt and Bishop get the expected results for situations that reflect acute needs, like energy expenditure or restoration or the immediate purging of an experience. They find no relations between situations and leisure choices for needs that presumably build over times greater than one day. Task generalization implies learning and frequent experiences, and compensation, as opposed to catharsis, may imply a long-term accommodation to individual needs. Thus, simply, acute needs may not be resolved by the leisure choice strategies of generalization or compensation, but chronic needs may.

The application of these theories or notions to children is difficult since in early childhood there is no clear-cut differentiation between work and play. The preschool child clearly lives within the constraints of a particular rearing-environment but the limitations do not prescribe specialized activities that will build needs for compensation in the sense of the theory. Also, there can be little generalization from one situation to another simply because the child lives in essentially one environment. In this setting if an activity is rewarding, the child will emit it more frequently there being no requirement to defer gratification.

The school child does live in the more complex situation of school and home and conceivably these ideas can explain play as generalization from or compensation for scholastic activity. In fact, Witty and Beaman (1933) found that the play behavior of mental deviates reflected directly the plays and games they had been taught at school. While this may be task generalization the similarity probably resulted from the paucity of options available to children lacking originality. The retardates probably played using skills and patterns taught them because they could not create original responses.

Early work involving compensation is summarized by Escalona (1943). She cited three separate studies concerning the capacity of an activity to substitute for another and satisfy the original intention. All three used a similar paradigm in a play-like situation. The subjects were allowed to start to play with a task that had a conclusion. They were then interrupted with the experimental substitute task, on completion of which they were free to return to the original task.

The frequency with which the subjects left the initial task unfinished, relative to a control group with no interpolated task, was taken as the degree to which the substitute task alleviated the need to complete the original task. Both children and adults showed that another task could satisfy the original intention. However, predicting which type of task had the capacity to reduce the tendency to resume the initial task was difficult. The compensatory substitutes were sometimes similar but often more difficult. Further, the specificity of intention, e.g., whether the subject intended to make a cat or merely an inanimate object from clay, the degree to which the function of the original object or task was defined, and the level of reality, all influenced the substitution value of the interpolated activity. No clear pattern emerged.

The work summarized by Escalona exemplifies the major problem for the generalization and compensation hypotheses: neither one is concerned specifically with particular tasks and short-term effects.   The common use of the concepts seems to apply to long-term predictions and has been motivated by the desire to plan for the exploitation or alleviation of psychic needs created by work.   When the concept of compensation is applied to acute rather than chronic situations then the distinction between the compensation, relaxation, and cathartic theories of play becomes blurred.   At this point the concepts of task generalization and compensation have not been clearly applied to the play of children and, apart from the limited application they might have to the school child, seem of limited value.

Cathartic Theories of Play

The concept of catharsis (from the Greek for purgation or purification) appeared in Aristotle's time when the ancient tragedies and some music were believed to purge the audience of their emotions.   The vicarious participation acted as some kind of release for emotional tension, enabling undesirable emotion to be released in a nondamaging way.   The idea was extended and applied to the play behavior of humans in the generally held view that play was an arena in which the emotions could be purged by activity with a reduced likelihood of damage.   Analogous to the surplus energy theory, this has been viewed as a hydraulic model. Life involves emotions associated with experiences and these seem to require release; otherwise their accumulation leads in some way to damage of the individual.   Giving vent to these feelings and emotions releases them as they build, thus safeguarding the integrity of the individual. This is the common view of catharsis and seemed to be the view of Groos in 1908 (Groos cited by Patrick, 1914) who extended his earlier view of play to account for the extensive fighting and aggressive plays in children.

The early meaning of the word, catharsis, was originally a general one, applying to the process whereby relief of any pent-up emotion or feeling was achieved by the exhibition of that emotion.   More recently, however, the concern for catharsis has been specifically directed towards aggressive behavior.   The apparent need for aggression to be released in a way that does not damage others has tended to limit the view of catharsis and the data available deal with it in this way.

> The idea of hostility catharsis is surely one of the most widely accepted doctrines in the folklore of both the man in the street and the social scientist.   For centuries, going back to Aristotle, people have believed that the exhibition of an emotion can "purge" an individual of that emotion. Contemporary formulations of this notion generally deal with anger and

aggressive behavior, and generally maintain that a person's hostile actions can reduce the strength of his aggressive tendencies, or somehow make him feel better. . . . In the psychological literature, at least, "catharsis" seems to refer most frequently to a lessening in the strength of the *instigation to aggression* supposedly produced by a hostile act [Berkowitz, 1964, p. 111].

This formulation says that the frustration engendered by the blocking of an intention to act can be relieved by allowing the subject to emit the act. In other words, it states only that the emission of the act satisfies the intention and is rewarding; but the notion that has sustained cathartic concepts of play has been an extension of this. The additional element which has not been justified is the assumption that it is possible to substitute socially acceptable behavior that relieves the tension associated with the blocking of the original socially unacceptable intention.

This extension has been seized by those concerned with recreation or sport as a justification for their activities, which they claimed allowed the purging of aggression in a regulated and harmless way.

For example, Menninger (1960) wrote:

Competitive games provide an unusually satisfactory social outlet for the instinctive aggressive drive. Psychiatrists postulate the existence in the personality of an aggressive energy drive, which constantly seeks expression. Where its direct expression is denied symptoms may develop. The most aggressive outlet is seen in those sports in which there is body movement . . . [p. 12].

Recently there has been a massive empirical attack on the concept of hostility and aggression catharsis. Catharsis is seen to grow from the concept of a completion tendency; the existence of a tension created by the lack of fulfillment of an intention. This is similar to the notion that underpinned the work on substitution activities (Escalona, 1943) but which is now typically limited to hostility and aggression. The intention to aggress against a tormentor leaves the subject under tension until he can injure the tormentor, see him injured, or relieve the tension by emitting a socially acceptable substitute, or catharsis.

Kenny (1953) in his doctoral dissertation tested the hypothesis that the expression of sanctioned aggression in a play situation would reduce the aggression in young children. The children were first given a story completion test that was scored for aggression. They were then divided into groups matched on aggression and allowed to play either in a setting that was neutral with respect to aggression with neutral toys, or in a setting designed to release aggression. Afterwards they were given a second story completion test to reveal the residual levels of aggression.

The results were opposite to what was predicted. The neutral or control group were diminished in aggressiveness as scored by the test, while the group given opportunities to purge their aggressions remained unchanged. Kenny concluded that the catharsis theory was not valid.

In the play situation some toys depend on the induction of apparent aggression by virtue of their design. For example, tanks, swords, handguns, etc., depend at least on aggressive displays for their use. Feshbach (1956) called this aggression *thematic aggression* since it depends on the essential play theme of the toy and the behavior in which it is embedded. Aggression between playmates that does not arise from the context he called *inappropriate aggression*. In an experiment designed to separate these kinds of aggression and test the catharsis hypothesis, boys and girls were first assessed over four months as to their inappropriate aggressiveness by classroom teachers. Then they were assigned as high aggression or low aggression children to one of three groups that either played with aggressive toys, played with neutral toys, or stayed in their classroom. During play the aggression was scored, and after the four-week duration of the experiment the children were rated again by the classroom teacher.

During the play sessions there was no clear evidence for a cathartic effect. In the aggressive toy group there should have been more thematic but less inappropriate aggression relative to the reference group. Although there were differences among the different age levels, the results were consistent—the aggressive toys induced more inappropriate aggression than did neutral toys. Further, in the long-term, some of the boys who were not aggressive before the play experience showed increased classroom ratings of aggression afterwards.

> [This] . . . raises a serious question regarding the validity of the widely held but by no means universal assumption that the expression of aggression in a socially approved form will reduce the amount of socially disapproved aggressive behavior [Feshbach, 1956, pp. 460–461].

Addressing the same question, Hokanson and Burgess (1962) showed that fantasy aggression which did not produce direct injury to the tormentor also did not produce a reduction in tension; similarly, neither did the opportunity to aggress against a substitute.

Berkowitz (1964) raises the issue that the potentially aggressive person will not necessarily become aggressive until appropriate cues are present. These cues are that aggression is sanctioned and that the original tormentor is in some way available to be aggressed against. When aggressive behavior is emitted there is a demonstrable reduction in arousal as measured by a variety of physiological measures. The encouragement to aggress, to allow the tormented one to "get it off his chest," seems to be one of the very circumstances or cues to aggressive action necessary to the build-up of the expectancy for aggression. It is this expectancy that when blocked causes the need to be aggressive. If the tormentor is in some way immune to aggression and/or aggression is not sanctioned, then the hostility of the tormented one wanes. Berkowitz and Green (1962) go on to raise the important point that when a person is allowed to aggress against a tormentor, it is possible that he will continue to aggress against him in the future when frustrated by him or someone else. In other words, aggression begets aggression.

The aggression research clearly questions whether substitute acts do reduce tension. It shows that anger must be present if the aggression is to reduce emotional and physiological tension. Further, the sanctioning of aggressive acts, be they verbal or a substitute, is likely to increase the level of aggression in children. However, it is not within the scope of this treatment to review in depth the hostility catharsis literature. This has been done by Berkowitz (1964), Berkowitz (1969), and Nighswander and Meyer (1969), and can be neatly summarized using the findings of Mallick and McCandless (1966):

1. Frustration leads to heightened aggressive feelings, but subsequent aggressive behavior does not reduce aggression.
2. Aggression without the existence of anger is without cathartic effect.
3. Reasonable interpretation of a frustrator's behavior is strikingly effective in reducing both behavioral and verbal aggression against him.
4. Verbal aggression towards a frustrator does not reduce aggression toward him, but may actually increase it [p. 596].

In the light of the spirited attack from those armed with data, the original simplistic concept of hostility catharsis and justifications like that of Menninger do not look promising. Catharsis as a process has probably always been a speculative notion growing from the need to control violent and disorganizing emotions. It has been convenient to assume that a hydraulic model can be extended to provide a safety valve of substitute action.

Psychoanalytic Theory of Play

The interest of psychoanalysts in play has led from the early observations of Freud, who concerned himself with play occasionally in his writings, to a clearly proposed explanation by Wälder (1933) and then to the more recent writings of Erikson (1950). In this theory concern for the individual behavior is clearly paramount. Much of the play of the child is seen as being motivated by the "pleasure principle" and acts are performed for the gratification they bring. The gratification is an affect accompanying the receipt of a reward. The reward can be extrinsic and lead to a tangible contingency or be intrinsic in that the activity itself is rewarding. The latter, called functional pleasure, is associated with mastering an element of the environment, and is a concept similar to that of Groos's "joy in being a cause" and the competence/effectance (mastery) motive of White (1959).

The "pleasure principle" is merely a Freudian restatement of one modern view of behavior which holds that the probability of responses being emitted is a function of previous reinforcement—the law of effect (see Kimble, 1961, p. 10). However, the psychoanalytic theory goes beyond the pleasure principle to explain the play of children that is related to real experiences that are not pleasant.

But before proceeding to the involvement of play in the psychic process of the child, some insight into those processes is necessary. Three processes, each possessing the capacity to influence behavior, or libidinal energy, exist in a person. These processes, the id, ego, and superego, compete for influence and unpleasant internal conflicts often result. The id represents the primitive pressures of our inheritance upon behavior. As Erikson (1950) puts it, "the id is the deposition in us of the whole of evolutionary history. The id is everything that is left in our organization of the responses of the amoeba and of the impulses of the ape . . .—everything that would make us 'mere creatures' [p. 167]." Opposite in polarity to the id is the superego. This process represents "the demands of our conscience," and is presumed to be a higher process reflecting our humanity and setting us apart from animals. Between the two lies the ego.

The ego balances the extreme demands of the opposing id and superego with its concern for reality. It represents a rational charting of a path for an individual through the maze of conflicts and constraints imposed by the real world outside. The problem besetting an individual during development is to develop an ego that can chart that path and resist the blandishments of the extremes. This process takes time. A neonate is seen as governed exclusively by its id. As experience is accumulated, a superego is developed along with an ego. As a result, mechanisms for balancing the id and superego are required by the developing ego. They are acquired to some extent during play.

Play is partially separated from reality and allows the child's ego freedom to bend with the demands of id and superego. The child can try out new balance points and mechanisms. The ego can be exercised and in so doing work out conflicts between id and superego. Play involves the acquisition of control by the ego and the amelioration of the effects of loss of control. In other words, play is a critical process for the development of ego strength in the normal child. The normal auto-therapeutic processes of play usually unfold continuously as the child develops and the psychoanalysts, exemplified by Erikson, see their theories as applicable to normal development.

In addition to their view of the normal, they are clinicians concerned with the extremes of behavior engendered by wild imbalances in the psychic processes. Thus they are concerned with case studies and using them to make inferences about what is normal. In fact, it is from the bizarre that they infer what is normal. Hence, there is an almost exclusively anecdotal system of reporting psychoanalytic thinking and a preoccupation with gross clinical abnormality. It is this clinical interest in the effects of unpleasant experiences that often extends their interest in play still further.

Children have but a tenuous mastery of the environment about them and in their experience it is confusing, complex, and difficult to master. Add to this a precarious balance between id and superego and it can be seen that the child frequently encounters experiences that he cannot control and that are unpleasant. Play and dreams have an autotherapeutic effect as originally explained by Freud.

> It is clear that in their play children repeat everything that has made a great impression on them in real life, and that in doing so they abreact the strength of the impression and, as one might put it, make themselves master of the situation. But on the other hand it is obvious that all their play is influenced by a wish that dominates them the whole time—the wish to be grown up and do what grown up people do. It can also be observed that the unpleasurable nature of an experience does not always unsuit it for play. If the doctor looks down a child's throat or carries out some small operation on him, we may be quite sure that these frightening experiences will be the subject of the next game; but we must not in that connection overlook the fact that there is a yield of pleasure from another source. As the child passes over from the passivity of the experience to the activity of the game, he hands on the disagreeable experience to one of his playmates and in this way revenges himself on a substitute [Freud, 1955, p. 16].

This notion of Freud's has some similarity with the notion of catharsis in that in some way the players divest themselves of an unpleasant affect. Later psychoanalytic theorists have taken the opposite view. The psychoanalytic process is concerned with the subject of the unpleasant experience and its residual negative affect trying to come to terms with or assimilate the unpleasantness. In other words, the original concept of catharsis or handing on the unpleasant affect does not explain the repetition of the play activity associated with an unpleasant experience. In the former case, once cathartic play is successful, the child should move on to another activity. However, repetition of the unpleasant experience is a process

> . . . by which excessive experiences are divided into small quantities, reattempted and assimilated in play. . . . Play may now be characterized as a method of constantly working over and, as it were, assimilating piecemeal an experience which was too large to be assimilated instantly at a swoop [Wälder, 1933, p. 217].

This gradual mechanism of assimilation is seen to serve the same purpose as the processes of mourning, fantasy, and nightmares in which the individual assimilates excessive experiences gradually.

Psychoanalytic theory also deals with the question of reality in the play of children and fantasy in adults, which are seen as similar processes.

> Might we not say that every child at play behaves like a creative writer, in that he creates a world of his own, or, rather, rearranges the things of his world in a new way which pleases him? It would be wrong to think he does not take his play seriously; on the contrary he takes his play very seriously and he expends large amounts of emotion on it. *The opposite of play is not what is serious but what is real.* In spite of all the emotion with which he cathects his world of play, the child distinguishes it quite well from reality; and he likes to link his imagined objects and situations to the tangible and visible things of the real world. This linking is all that differentiates the child's "play" from "phantasying" [Freud, 1959, pp. 143–144].

Psychoanalytic theory in summary suggests that children consciously add actual elements from their environment to their fantasies, mixing reality and unreality into their play. Adults are seen as experientially and societally more constrained, emphasizing their grasp of reality, and hiding their tendency to deal with unreality in their play. Thus, adults are left with covert fantasy.

Freud was much concerned with children's needs to transpose their roles in experience from passivity to activity. Things are done to the child and he exhibits no control or mastery. From this stems the desire to be grown-up and exert control. It explains why in play passive experiences are converted into active ones, why much play is imitative of adult roles where control is exhibited. Accordingly, authority figures, controllers of people, and operators, controllers of machines and things, should feature frequently in children's fantasy plays.

Finally, the most important element in the psychoanalytic conception of the child and play is the capacity for the repetition in play of prior unpleasant and excessive experiences to diminish their residual impact and allow the child to assimilate or come to terms with them. This notion is used in two ways by those concerned with treating children emotionally disturbed by previous experiences. In diagnosis the repeated elements of the play suggest the traumatic experience, and in habilitation, children are given opportunities to assimilate them.

The three elements together explain why the incidence of play diminishes with age. As the child grows older, the environment becomes less confounded and confusing, and the child has greater control over it. Therefore, the incidence of excessive and unpleasant experiences to be assimilated diminishes, and the need for play is reduced. However, this does not account for play behavior maintained by the pleasure principle, and it may be that the incidence of that class of play responses may not diminish with age or is only constrained by other limitations such as the necessity for work and/or reduced vigor.

Gilmore (1966a) lumps cathartic theory and psychoanalytic theories together, claiming that the psychoanalytic theory is merely a special case of the cathartic theory. The assumption that they are essentially one and the same process leads to difficulties although perhaps not for psychoanalysts.

> The term catharsis was introduced into psychiatry by Sigmund Freud and Josef Breuer to describe a method of treatment by which hysterical patients, under hypnosis, relived, or at least remembered, the circumstances under which their symptoms originated, expressed the emotion accompanying those circumstances and were thus relieved of the symptoms. Though the term (sometimes used synonymously with abreaction) is no longer in common use among psychiatrists, the idea is in fact a major component of the theory and practice of psychoanalysis [Anonymous, 1968].

Although the outcomes of the two mechanisms may be the same in that the subject is relieved of the tension, the procedures seem opposite in action. In catharsis theory the emotion is vented by visiting the aggression on the tormentor or some substitute, whereas in the psychoanalytic model described here the child assimilates his emotion by repeating it in a non-serious setting.

Play Therapy

Growing from the psychoanalytic theory and cathartic theories is play therapy, which exploits play as a natural situation for children to express themselves. Play therapy

> . . . may be described as an opportunity that is offered to the child to experience growth under the most favorable conditions. Since play is his

natural medium for self-expression, the child is given the opportunity to play out his accumulated feelings of tension, frustration, insecurity, aggression, fear, bewilderment, confusion.

By playing out these feelings he brings them to the surface, gets them out in the open, faces them, learns to control them, or abandons them [Axline, 1947, p. 16].

Play therapy seems to be a mixture of mechanisms which encourages children to divest themselves of negative affects by handing them on by purging or transferring them, and a process whereby they are assimilated (Freud, 1946; Klein, 1955). Cathartic theory and psychoanalytic theory's opposite mechanisms seem to have been embedded in play therapy. There is no data that serves to differentiate when one mechanism will be used rather than the other, nor is there any data, apart from anecdotes from clinical settings, concerning the efficacy of either mechanism.

It is difficult to evaluate catharsis and assimilation as mechanisms contributing to the psychic adjustment or mental health of children. The theoretical tenets are steeped in a clinical tradition and it is difficult to assign degrees of success or failure of therapeutic experiences systematically. Secondly, the case histories have reported only those children who have failed to use their autotherapeutic mechanisms effectively during their maturation and have thus become medical problems.

The empirical work on hostility catharsis suggests that perhaps the confidence in catharsis as a mechanism is unfounded As yet there has been little research that bears on the assimilative aspect of the mixture. Finally, both concepts are presumed to explain behavior that is not accounted for by the concepts of reward. The play behavior of concern seems beyond the "pleasure principle" and is thereby limited. The challenge is for the supporters of the single cathartic theory or the double-barrelled cathartic-assimilatory theory to develop evidence that the formulations have demonstrable explanatory or predictive power.

A formal empirical study which bears on the psychoanalytic theory has been done by Gilmore (1966b). One facet of his series of three studies concerned the notion that when anxious a child will prefer to play with items which are salient to that anxiety. This action allows the child mastery over the anxiety invoking experiences and a reduction in the psychic tension they create. As an additional feature Gilmore also expected that when children were not anxious they would prefer to play with toys that were novel; this was justified by Piagetian theory (Piaget, 1962), namely "assimilation," covered later in this chapter.

The first study involved children in hospitals with the salient toys being hospital related items such as toy stethoscopes, etc., and the novel or complex toys being unrelated to the hospital setting. On the grounds of the psychoanalytic theory as predicted, the hospitalized children preferred to play with toys relevant to their situations.

The other two studies were experimental in that the subjects were normal school children who were made anxious by the prospect of a painful initiation in a secret society. While waiting for initiation, which the experimenter told the subjects would involve a painful noise or painful light, the children were allowed to play with carefully selected toys among which were some relevant to the impending visual and auditory stimuli. The children were then let into the secret that there was no initiation at all, and then they played again. The results were not clear-cut. Gilmore concluded that preference for novel objects did not change very much with changes in anxiety although greater anxiety produced a tendency to play more with novel items. However, anxiety influenced the kind of toy chosen. The anxious child is either markedly more interested or markedly less interested in the anxiety relevant item. Gilmore cannot explain this but feels that the effect is a function of degree of fear. Mildly anxious children play with the anxiety relevant object, but highly anxious children avoid it.

The importance of these studies lies in the demonstration that with ingenuity it is possible to test empirically a postulate of the psychoanalytic theory. The outcomes were some weak support for the notion that anxiety relevant toys would be played with by mildly anxious subjects as claimed by the psychoanalytic theory.

Psychoanalytic aspects of play have not been treated extensively here. The reason is simply my inability to grasp any essential and rigorous thread to the arguments of the psychoanalysts. The orientation of this book to play is a behavioral one dealing with theoretical formulations and data bearing on them. In contrast to this thrust the essence of psychoanalysis seems subjective rather than scientific. Having revealed my biases, it seems that psychoanalytic theories have been ill-formulated and that there has been almost no attempt to establish ways of testing them.

The psychoanalytic writings and reports are essentially subjective interpretations of what the analyst thought the motives for the play behavior of the patient might be. Even Erikson (1950) seriously doubts the validity of the assumption that play behavior means anything more than that the child happened to do something in a certain way. He questions the interpretability of play responses, calling for great care in assuming that play has a meaning beyond itself. The only point where he sees this as justifiable is when the play is sufficiently bizarre to warrant attention. This of course requires a clear view of what is normal in a setting, which it would seem that play therapists probably do not have. However, to allow the readers some opportunity to formulate their own opinions, entry into the psychoanalytic literature on play can be gained via the following references (Alexander, 1958; Erikson, 1950; Freud, A., 1946; Klein, 1948, 1955; Lebo, 1955; Moustakas, 1959; Dorfman, 1951).

Cognitive Dynamics and Play

Piaget (Flavell, 1963) has been the major worker postulating that children's behavior depends upon their cognitive structures. He argues that as time passes and experience accumulates there are important changes in the way children perceive and think about the real world around them. As children mature they move through a series of identifiable phases and their behavior and its changes allow inferences as to their causes. Thus, children play (or behave) in certain ways because that kind of behavior is determined by the structure of the thinking or cognitive processes of the child.

The structure of thinking is presumed to be inherited. The processes of intelligence are "wired-into" the neural structure of people, and the interaction of that fixed structure with the environment determines the essential human nature of the thinking. Thus, for Piaget, the crucial effects of behavior, including play, are worked upon the thinking of the child rather than the environment. Play takes place in the mind, with the body involved in process as a producer of effects or inputs for further thinking.

When a neonate, the child lives in the world of minimal order, where there are few responses available to him and sensory input is a mélange of stimuli from the self and from the surroundings. At first there is no differentiation between self and environment, but the child possesses sequences of actions, like sucking and grasping, that Piaget calls *schemas*. The organized actions are similar to the *plans* and *strategies* of Miller, Galanter, and Pribram (1960) and lead to interactions between the child, his body, and the surroundings. In so doing they produce effects on existing schemata, eventually lead to further schemata and a beginning to differentiation between self and environment. As children become older they also develop strategies for thinking about the sensory data they are currently receiving, and have received in the past. These organized strategies for dealing with mental events are cognitive schemata, and they naturally become increasingly complex with age.

The motives for children's engagement with thinking about their world is claimed to be an instinct or inherent tendency (Maier, 1965) to balance external reality and internal affect. Individuals try to maintain an equilibrium between reality and feeling in the face of changes in themselves and in the environment. This kind of formulation reveals Piaget's early links with psychoanalytic models of the world. While it may provide a convenient handle for thinking about development and behavior, it ultimately begs the question of why the person would strive for this balance. The claiming of an instinct suffers exactly the same limitations that early instinct theories suffer. What Piaget seems to be saying is that since people appear to strive for this balance there must be a mechanism governing it, and it can be called an instinct. Even though Piaget does not seem to attempt to delineate a mechanism driving the cognitive behavior of people, he does deal powerfully with the patterns of behavior and thinking that the undefined instinctual mechanisms produce.

Piaget established four major phases in the development of the child: sensorimotor (birth to two years), pre-operational (two to seven years), concrete operations (seven to eleven years) and, finally, a stage of formal operations. These stages merge into one another as the cognitive style of the child changes. At first the child's thinking is limited to the manipulation of sensory input and does not involve symbols. After about two years the child acquires symbolic functioning without the presence of the object. He can imitate previous events, can search for objects and begin to perceive the constraints of reality. However, the child does not go beyond the concrete. Next, the child proceeds to manipulate symbols, to classify, to comprehend number, weight, volume, time, space. Finally the child thinks as an adult.

These developments in the cognitive functioning must influence the child's play. The child reorders the schemata of the preceding stages, becoming more complex with time. For example, deferred imitation should not appear before the second stage, and word plays and jokes that depend on reversals and transformations of symbols should not appear before the third. Thus, the content of play and its ordering is susceptible to analysis in the Piagetian tradition.

As the child becomes more organized the two major ingredients of Piaget's model become apparent. These are the processes of assimilation and accommodation that are eventually to form the basis of intelligence. Assimilation is a process whereby:

> Every encounter with an environmental object necessarily involves some kind of cognitive structuring (or restructuring) of that object in accord with the nature of the organism's existing intellectual organization [Flavell, 1963, p. 48].

Thus, children impose on reality their own construction or interpretation of it. Children impose on reality the constraints of their own schemata and experience.

In opposition to this is the process of accommodation whereby children alter their schemata, cognitive and sensorimotor, to meet the intransigent demands of reality. Thus, children, presumably as a result of interpreting the feedback created by their interactions with the real world of their bodies and surroundings, are required to modify their own thoughts and behaviors.

These two processes operate together to produce the adaptation of children to their niches in the environment. Although at one time or another the behavior might show bias toward assimilation or accommodation, they are part and parcel of one process and do not exist in isolation. To explain, Flavell (1963, p. 49) cites Piaget.

> . . . From the beginning assimilation and accommodation are indissociable from each other. Accommodation of mental structures to reality implies the existence of assimilatory schemata apart from which any structure would be impossible. Inversely, the formation of schemata through assimilation entails the utilization of external realities to which the former must accommodate, however crudely. . . .
>
> Assimilation can never be pure because by incorporating new elements into its earlier schemata the intelligence constantly modified the latter in order to adjust them to new elements. Conversely, things are never known by themselves, since this work of accommodation is only possible as a function of the inverse process of assimilation.

The balance between accommodation and assimilation is seen as the basis for intelligence. The demands of the here and now reality are balanced by the consideration of the structure or laws induced into previous experiences. Thus, new or creative responses are possible; the perceived constraints of the surroundings are not binding, and yet the respondent balances the likelihood of the desired outcomes on the basis of generalized previous experiences or data.

The equilibrium between assimilation and accommodation is not static. As individuals experience events their cognitive structure increases in complexity, they accommodate their thinking to account for more experiences. Children progressively modify their expectations or hypotheses as to outcomes and cognitive strategies to fit their sense data better. As the cognitive and sensorimotor schemata change, different constructs of the real world are created. Thus, over time there is a process of increasing intellectual grasp of reality. Change in assimilatory processes produces new accommodations, and the accommodatory changes alter the cognitive schemata and the assimilatory constraints placed on immediate experience. The individual's complexity spirals upward over time as assimilation and accommodation interact.

> In summary, the functional characteristics of the assimilatory and accommodatory mechanisms are such that the possibility of cognitive change

is insured, but the magnitude of any given change is always limited. The organism adapts repeatedly, and each adaptation necessarily paves the way for its successor. Structures are not infinitely modifiable however, and not everything which is potentially assimilable can in fact be assimilated by an organism at point X in his development. On the contrary, the subject can incorporate only those components of reality which its on-going structure can assimilate without drastic change [Flavell, 1963, p. 50].

In addition, Piaget suggests that although chronic equilibrium between the twin mechanisms exists, there are acute disturbances of the equilibrium when assimilatory behavior preempts accommodation and vice versa. The behavior that occurs during the times when assimilation predominates can be described as playful, and that when accommodation predominates as imitative. Thus, in Piagetian terms, whether behavior is playful, adaptive, or imitative depends on the interaction between the twin mechanisms.

Play is characterized by the assimilation of elements in the real world without the balancing constraint of accepting the limitations of accommodating to them.

In play the primary object is to mold reality to the whim of the cognizer, in other words, to assimilate reality to various schemas with little concern for precise accommodation to that reality. Thus, as Piaget put it, in play there is "primacy of assimilation over accommodation" [Flavell, 1963, p. 65].

The primacy of accommodation, however, leads to imitation where the imitator is concerned with taking exact account of the reality of the imitated. The existing structure of the imitator is subordinated to the structure of the thing imitated At this point in his explication of Piaget's thinking, Flavell (1963) branched to an example presented by Piaget and so shall we.

. . . intelligence tends towards permanent equilibrium between assimilation and accommodation. For instance, in order to draw an objective towards him by means of a stick, the child must assimilate both stick and objective to the schema of prehension and that of movement through contact, and he must also accommodate these schemas to the objects, their length, distance, etc., in accordance with the causal order hand-stick-objective. Imitation, on the contrary, is the continuation of accommodation . . . to which it subordinates assimilation. For instance, imitation will reproduce the motion made by the stick in reaching the objective, the movement of the hand thus being determined by those of the stick and the objective (which is by definition accommodation), without the hand actually affecting the objects (which would be assimilation).

There is, however, a third possibility, that of assimilation *per se*. Let us assume, for instance, that the stick does not reach its objective and that the child consoles himself by hitting something else, or that he suddenly becomes interested in moving the stick for its own sake, or that when he has no stick he takes a piece of paper and applies the schema of the stick to it for fun. In such cases there is a kind of free assimilation, without accommodation to spatial conditions or to the significance of the objects. This is simply play, in which reality is subordinated to assimilation which is distorted, since there is no accommodation. Intelligent adaptation, imitation and play are thus the three possibilities, and they result according as there is stable equilibrium between assimilation and accommodation or primacy of one of these two tendencies over the other [Piaget, 1962, pp. 85–86].

Sutton-Smith (1966) raised many objections to this theory, most of which were immediately repudiated by Piaget (1966). An important argument remained, however. Sutton-Smith pointed out that play and imitation as opposites were created by a disequilibrium in the assimilatory and accommodatory components of intelligent adaptation. Piaget's theory claimed that, as the child develops, the imbalances that detracted from intelligent functioning would diminish. Thus, since play and imitation do not occur during intelligent adaptation, as intelligence increases, in both efficiency and adequacy with experience, play and presumably imitation will become less important. Sutton-Smith goes on to criticize Piagetian theory at each of the various stages in the development of the child, developing a theme that play remains important, does not become more realistic or rationalistic as intelligence develops, but remains symbolic, ritualistic, playful, even into adulthood.

Piaget (1962) suggested that as a result of the increased cognitive complexity of the child resulting from development, the complexity of play would increase with time. This complexity would take the form of constraints or rules imposed on the activity, such that their difficulty increased and competition became possible. "Games with rules . . . increase in number, both absolutely and relatively, with age. They are almost the only ones that persist at the adult stage [1962, p. 146]." Eifermann (1971), in using data from what must be the largest observational study undertaken on play, quarrels convincingly with Piaget on this point. Using a carefully selected sample of schools representing the cultural, religious, and geographic entities in Israel, and an army of 150 observers, she studied the play and games of small groups of children. She reports very clear patterns. Participation in rule-governed competitive games increased in popularity to a peak at fourth grade. After that time participation in these activities dropped steeply towards adolescence and beyond.

Eifermann attempts to explain the differences between her findings and Piaget's by noting that rule-governed behavior may not always be competitive. There were many occasions when children would generate and apply rules to noncompetitive behaviors. The accommodation/ assimilation model suggests that competitive and rule-governed behaviors particularly in a social setting are accommodatory and lead to increased capacity of children and their schemas to deal with the realities of their social setting. Piaget claims that rule-governed games increase with age, yet as the children become skilled socially, their need for agreed schemata to govern social settings should diminish. This is just what Eifermann found. After a phase in which children's interest in these activities rose to a peak at the fourth or fifth grade level, the trend reversed. After the peak, preference for non-rule-oriented practice and symbolic activities increased with age.

Eifermann suggests a new factor, that she claimed was ignored by Piaget, to account for the changes. She called this factor "challenge," which represents the balance between a child's intentions and the possible outcomes of responding. Challenge requires the running of moderate risks in attempts to produce outcomes. The uncertainty inherent in traversing from response to outcome is motivating in itself, and sustains much of the behavior of older children. They do not need explicit rules and competitions to govern their play behavior. Challenge can be construed as closely related to conceptions of impact in the theory characterizing play as arousal-seeking behavior. Maier claims that Piaget saw play as ludic "activity calculated to amuse and to excite the playing individual [1965, p. 105]." Challenge results in the excitement of the individual; it is arousing. Amusement, presumably resulting from humor, is also arousing, and was something that Eifermann ignored.

The concepts of amusement and excitation are critical ones. They are to surface again in Chapter 5 where exactly the mechanism that is missing from Piaget's theories is postulated. The apparent conflict between Eifermann and Piaget can be resolved if the motive for engagement with the environment is taken to be a need for stimulation provided by the processing of information. Piaget assumes that play behavior will only retain its stimulating nature if it is complexified by rules and competitions. Eifermann shows that preference for competition and rules drops rapidly after the fifth or sixth grade. It may be that children by that time have become sufficiently organized to allow increasingly complex manipulations of syntactic, cultural, and experiential structures or roles to allow for their manipulation and the production of humor.

Providing that a basic mechanism can be supplied to drive the interaction of accommodation and assimilation, then Piaget's developmental phases can be integrated into a theory of behavior. At the moment,

Piaget knows that children advance through phases as a result of their searching for balance. He can't say why, beyond that this advance is instinctual. When such a mechanism for driving the child into engagements with the environment is built, then the worth of Piaget's developmentalism can be realized. The mechanism waits in Chapter 5, and an integration is attempted in Chapter 6.

Play as Learned Behavior

Long ago, Thorndike (Kimble, 1961, p. 10) advanced his "law of effect" which in essence claims that a response has an increased probability of emission if it is accompanied by a pleasant or reinforcing event and a decreased probability of occurring if the consequence is unpleasant. Since then psychologists have built an impressive body of theories concerning the nature of learning and the dependence of behavior in general on learning. The old polemic of nature versus nurture, or instinct versus learning, has been played down of late. The age of grand theoretical systems of instincts on the one hand and the learning theories on the other has given way now to an essentially atheoretical empirical phase in which the relations between phenomena are charted. However, there remain strong derivatives of the "law of effect" which, having resisted the tests of time, sustain a powerful view of behavior as determined largely by learning.

Play as a subset of behavior can be reduced to the simple connections of stimulus-response psychology. This view of play is not customarily conceived as a theory and learning has not been formally presented as an explanation for play. However, play can be explained as merely learned behavior called forth by the contingencies surrounding the player and is therefore subject to the broader theories of learning. The notion fits well into a determinist system in which all acts are seen as motivated. The stimuli calling forth the response presumably can be classified into serious or critical to survival or not. Responses to critical stimuli would be work and responses to other stimuli, presumably play. Thus, play is behavior made in response to stimuli in the environment that is not demonstrably critical for survival. In both work and play particular responses are influenced by the outcomes of previous responses to the same or similar stimuli. Thus, children's play responses are learned as a result of their experiences.

In fact, this position does not require the differentiation of the behavior of the organism into work or play. The identification of the stimulus-response connection is sufficient. This view is a powerful one. It takes into account individual differences in experience and constitution by charting which stimuli are connected to a contingency or outcome by means of a response. Some contingencies are seen as increasing the probability of a specific response, in which case they are positive reinforcers, and in the opposite case they are negative.

The interplay of positive and negative reinforcers on the behavior of a child are often clearly demonstrable in a formal setting or when the outcomes are critical for survival. Children learn rapidly to emit responses on which food, warmth, etc., are contingent. These reinforcers are primary. Their immediate and potent effects are readily charted. However, in reality the contingencies operating are more often blurred. The determination of which primary reinforcer is operating is confused because at any one time several contingencies overlap.

A major source of complexity arises from the association of other events in time with the occurrence of primary reinforcement. These other events take on by association some of the valency of the accompanying reinforcer. Thus, for example, secondary stimulus events consistently associated with feeding come eventually to produce similar responses in the absence of the original feeding stimulus. This secondary reinforcement plays a crucial role in maintaining learned behavior in the absence of a primary reinforcer.

Presumably these secondary reinforcers can be chained through experience and secondary reinforcers can influence the probability of responses, even when the connection to the original reinforcer is not clear. These secondary reinforcers are of critical importance in understanding human behavior. From the first consummatory responses of the neonate at the breast, primary drive reduction is embedded in a complex of contiguous stimulus events. The smiles, movements, and crooning of the mother after a while take on reinforcing power in their own right, and vest in her the power to modify the behavior of the child. In the same way a host of other stimuli from other humans and the environment eventually join in the interactions between the child, its responses and their consequences.

This view of play as learned behavior sees the structure of children's behavior as a reflection of the organization of the contingencies around them. Many of these contingencies, negative and positive, are mediated by means of secondary social reinforcers, the smiles or the threats of the humans surrounding the child. The influence of selective disbursement of secondary reinforcers on the behavior of the child is extensive.

Since the selective disbursement of these reinforcers is under the control of a human, attempts are made to direct the behavior of another in a way that produces counter-reinforcement. More simply exemplified, adults selectively reinforce behavior in the child that is reinforcing to them. What is reinforcing to each adult will have been embedded in the roots of his own experience. Some attributes will be unique to the individual but others will be experiences common to a race, a class, a religion, a nation, or a location. The combination of these divisions in experience common to a group sets its behavior apart to some extent—it forms a culture or subculture.

The culture at the macroscopic end and perhaps simply the family life-style at the microscopic, influence subtly but extensively the reinforcers operating on a child. To the extent that children's behavior is learned, then it is potently influenced by the complex of secondary reinforcers erected by their parents and other adults and children occupying the same cultural and environmental niche.

A major theorist whose work has dealt specifically with this is Sutton-Smith. He has long been involved in the study of cultural differences and their effects on the play of children old enough to cooperate together to play games (Sutton-Smith, 1951). Sutton-Smith proposed and provided data to support his hypothesis that the child-rearing practices of various cultures would reflect the essential characteristics of the culture. These rearing patterns in themselves would create stresses and the children would compensate for them by playing games that predominantly relieved their stress. In turn, the playing of these games would aid in the process of enculturation of the child—society's goal. He termed this the conflict-enculturation hypothesis.

Roberts and Sutton-Smith (1962) formulated and tested the conflict-enculturation hypothesis by studying the differences in rearing patterns and games played by the children in three societies for which both sets of data were available. The children's games were classified into those requiring as the essential ingredients strategy, skill, or luck. The rearing patterns could likewise be categorized in terms of emphasis on obedience, responsibility, or achievement. Clear evidence was found for an association between the predominance of one type of game and a particular emphasis in the rearing patterns in the ethnographer's descriptions of the social structures of the societies studied.

The researchers reported their analysis in considerable detail, looking at the possible combinations of rearing patterns and game structure. However, for simplicity, relationships have been stylized and the major findings seemed to be as follows:

Societies that reared their children for responsibility, or inculcated the necessity of routines that allowed little scope for individuality or creative problem-solving also seemed to have a reverence for the intervention of divine gods. The rearing patterns required the children not to reason but to do as they were told exactly. Life was humdrum responsibility. As a result, the children saw little opportunity to exert control over their circumstances and improvements in their circumstances were due to luck.

In this atmosphere games of chance predominated as reflections of how the society structured the lives of its members. To quote Roberts and Sutton-Smith:

> According to this interpretation, a game of chance is a response to the passivity of the players' normal life role and an expression of incompatible responses toward irresponsibility which are in conflict with the diligent role of the responsible provider. Benevolent fate, if not fantasy, may lift the worker out of his or her life tasks with magical efficacy [1962, p. 179].

In societies valuing achievement or performance, games of physical skill seemed to reflect this concern directly. When the rearing system consistently valued achievement, pressuring the child consistently in terms of his performance, it was presumed to generate anxiety concerning performance. This anxiety is assuaged by the participation in games of skill where the arbiter is relative performance. However, in games the outcome is less critical, and the children can come to terms with, or assimilate, their anxiety concerning the achievement and frequency of achievement in the arena of play.

The third relationship seemed to exist between games of strategy and emphasis of the rearing patterns on obedience. Obedience training tended to require a severity on the part of the rearers towards those in whom obedience is to be inculcated. The child has his own wishes and individuality subverted by the aversive consequences of not obeying the authority figure. This is presumed to generate aggressive tendencies in circumstances where aggression is actively discouraged. Roberts and Sutton-Smith argue that these conflicts are displaced and appear in games where there are opportunities to control others and where stylized but attenuated aggression forms the substance of the game. These games then provide opportunities to force obedience on others and thereby allow the players to eliminate or reduce their aggressive and hostile feelings induced by the rearing pressures.

No one simple model was used to explain these relationships. The three major associations between game predominance and rearing pattern were explained separately. The relation between the predominance of games of skill in high-achieving societies was explained as generalization. Anxiety concerning achievement is reflected in the games. However, the other two relationships seem to be indirect. In some societies children are trained to feel a responsibility for following the recipes of life which preempts the requirement for them to behave adaptively from first principles. There is an abdication of control to a god or a procedure, and as a result major changes in circumstances occur fortuitously.

Thus, games of chance appear in situations where life is in the hands of routine or the god. Strategic games seem to derive from the need to compensate for the indignities of being obedient. Games, a setting apart from the requirements of obedience, are presumed to allow for the expression of mastery over events and to purge aggressive and hostile feelings in a noncritical situation.

As a result of the game activities, the children are seen as being better able to deal with the stresses imposed on them during their rearing and thus more effectively enculturated.

This hypothesis was tested in a further setting by Roberts, Sutton-Smith, and Kendon (1963). They studied folk tales of games and complexity of societies described by ethnographers. There seemed to be a clear increase in games of strategy as the society became more complex. Strategic games were associated with political complexity, advanced agriculture, technology, and jurisdictional systems. They went on to arrange child-rearing patterns in order as they were allied with the emergence of complex cultures. In the first stage rearing required merely nurturance and self-reliance and generated no games. At the next stage societies reared for independence, responsibility, and achievement which gave rise to games of skill and to games of chance. Finally, at the highest level, obedience became necessary and with it games of strategy.

This study of rearing and subcultural differences has to be extended to the differences that exist between the sexes as a result of differences in rearing patterns (Sutton-Smith, Rosenberg & Morgan, 1963; Sutton-Smith, 1965), and to adults (Sutton-Smith, Roberts & Kozelka, 1963) and children in different classes in the United States. Here the game involvement followed the models of conflict/enculturation hypothesis where there were systematic subcultural differences in the rearing patterns of different classes of the society.

It is possible to predict that the family, influenced as they are by their subcultural circumstances, will, in turn, by the manipulation of the contingencies under their control, influence their children. The children will learn which behaviors are available to them, and the conflict/enculturation hypothesis goes some way in explaining what their game preferences will be once they are old enough to enter into cooperatively competitive games as children and adults. The conflict/enculturation hypothesis points to the interaction between the personality of the gamester (Sutton-Smith's word) and the demands of the rearing environment as the motive for the playing of games. The mismatch according to these sub-models results in differing game preferences and game playing. In this way the concept of play as a learned response is elaborated to take into account the processes of response generalization and compensation or catharsis. Sutton-Smith's theories are in the process of elaboration and further empirical test at this time but they seem to synthesize much of the work reported in this chapter.

Eifermann's (1971) massive study produced vast numbers of observations of play that allowed reliable comparisons of the way differences in play were manifested in differing locations like the kibbutz or in town, and in Arab or Israeli settings. She used these differences skillfully to test the conflict/enculturation hypothesis, among many others.

Eifermann interprets the hypothesis to mean that since rural children have better opportunities to participate in the work of a less competitive adult world than do their urban counterparts, they should exhibit fewer conflicts and therefore less interest in competitive games. She proceeded to test this using data to compare urban and rural play styles. With the exception of an Arab village school, Jewish country children exhibited more competitive play than their urban counterparts.

Eifermann claims that the conflict notion may need revision but the enculturative elements of the theory seemed sound. Competitiveness is a central feature of urban and Western society. In these settings competition and the status that ensues from success places considerable stress on the child. She argues that this is strongest in urban settings and preparation for adulthood in an urban setting creates mechanisms for dealing with that stress. Acculturation to competition should best take place in settings where there is reasonable chance of success and where failure is less critical. These requirements are met most satisfactorily for children in play groups that are of similar age. This being true, then urban children should play in age groups significantly more often than kibbutz children. They do. In town the homogeneity of the age groups remains uniformly high as the children grow older, whereas in the country that homogeneity has dropped markedly by the seventh or eighth grade. Presumably the stresses of enculturation are ended earlier by the smoother transition into the adult world that occurs in the country.

Subcultural differences in the play of American children have also been reported by Bishop and Chace (1971), who examined the kinds of rearing environments provided by parents with differing orientations to the world. Parents that were abstract thinkers independent of rules and recipes for dealing with events, set up an environment that was flexible, tolerated individuality, did not stereotype girls and boys, and produced children capable of dealing with greater complexity, lack of routine, and greater creativity in a laboratory play setting. The relationships to be expected from a generalization of a particular rearing style to the behavior of the children were found. Other class differences in play are beginning to be reported even for very young children. For example, Messer and Lewis (1970) found class and sex differences in the activity of toddlers, their independence from the mother, and their toy preferences in a play setting.   Middle-class boys showed greater activity and independence, and middle-class children showed greater preferences for manipulable toys, than did lower-class children.

Sutton-Smith and his collaborators have restricted themselves to games, or activities with stylized procedures and outcomes agreed upon by the participants, and have had considerable success.   But in so doing they had to exclude other play behaviors, and the content of these behaviors is proving difficult to quantify and research.   However, the more global but less useful application of simple learning theories to those behaviors must suffice at this time.

This view of play as learned responding is all-encompassing to the point where a primary or secondary reinforcer can be demonstrated to be maintaining the response.   For the theorist there is a comforting presence of a motive or cause for the behavior.   The organism is behaving in such a way as to maximize the probability of a positive payoff in the near future, or to minimize the probability of an aversive outcome.   Thus, play, like work, is subject to rewards and punishments and children will in the end play appropriately to gain the former and avoid the latter.

In some circumstances an act seems to be emitted without reference to a response contingency.   There are clearly behaviors that are difficult to chain to contingencies.   The responses which seem to be nonutilitarian in the sense that there is apparently no ultimate payoff are difficult to explain.   Play seems to contain many such behaviors.   This raises a difficulty for S-R psychologists because of the contention that all behavior is motivated.   The question is, "How to explain the unmotivated playful act?"   The difficulty is resolved by claiming that there really is a motive for the behavior.   The contingencies are merely hidden as yet and eventually sophisticated analysis will reveal them.   Examples of just this kind of argument are raised in the following chapter, where play is characterized as either motivated by stimulus-seeking, or by competence-effectance motivation in which, in both cases, the contingencies or reinforcers are claimed to come from within the organism itself.

Overview

The more recent the explanation for play, and probably for all phenomena, the more difficult it is to deal with conceptually.   The older theories have been winnowed by time.   They have been divested of qualifications and constraints, and invested with parsimony.   They have been simplified and the source material has been compacted.   The recent theories have not been extant long enough for this process to take place.   The relevant material is widespread and in some cases not yet incorporated into the secondary sources of reviews and texts. Consequently, this chapter on recent theories has more of the tone and flavor of the process whereby theories wax and wane.

For example, the generalization and compensation hypotheses are treated here simply because there are views at present that these processes really do govern leisure. The psychoanalytic school of thought exists and has been applied to play, with and without the age-old concept of catharsis. Piaget is still a powerful force and the application of learning theory to play as yet is associated with no particular theorist. All the notions presented above are at last giving rise to empirical tests, and in many years, after many data have been processed, some of the recent ideas may become quaint and of historical import only. Meanwhile they are contenders in the race to explain an important aspect of human behavior —play.

Table 4.1

Recent Theories of Play

NAME	PLAY IS CAUSED:	THIS EXPLANATION ASSUMES THAT:	IT CAN BE CRITICIZED BECAUSE:
6. Generalization	by the players using in their play experiences that have been rewarding at work	1. there are at least two separable categories of behavior 2. the players transfer to play or leisure, behaviors that are rewarded in another setting 3. to be useful we understand what rewards individuals at work	1. it seems to exclude play of preschool children 2. it assumes that at least some aspects of work are rewarding
7. Compensation	by players using their play to satisfy psychic needs not satisfied in or generated by the working behaviors	1. there are at least two separable categories of behavior 2. the player avoids in play or leisure behaviors that are unsatisfying in the work setting experiences that meet his psychic needs 3. to be useful we understand the mismatch of needs and satisfactions in the work setting (or vice versa)	1. it seems to exclude play of preschool children 2. it assumes that work is damaging or does not satisfy some needs
8. Catharsis	in part by the need to express disorganizing emotions in a harmless way by transferring them to socially sanctioned activity. This concept has been limited almost entirely to questions of aggression, and will be so here	1. frustration of an intention engenders hostility towards the frustrator 2. this frustration or hostility can be redirected to another activity 3. this hostility must be expressed to reduce psychic and physiological stress	1. it is a partial explanation for only the compensatory behavior engendered by hostility 2. the data show conclusively that sanctioning aggression increases it 3. the planning of activities to provide outlets for aggression constitutes its sanctioning

Theory			
9a. Psychoanalytic: I	in part by the players repeating in a playful form strongly unpleasant experiences, thereby reducing their seriousness and allowing their assimilation	1. stimulating unpleasant experiences in another setting reduces the unpleasantness of their residual effects	Both I and II ignore play that is not presumed to be motivated by the need to eliminate the products of strongly unpleasant experiences.
9b. Psychoanalytic: II	in part by the player during play reversing his role as the passive recipient of strong unpleasant experience, and actively mastering another recipient in a similar way, thus purging the unpleasant effects	1. achieving mastery, even in a simulated experience, allows the elimination of the products of unpleasant experience by passing similar experiences on to other beings or objects	
10. Developmental	by the way in which a child's mind develops. Thus play is caused by the growth of the child's intellect and is conditioned by it. Play occurs when the child can impose on reality his own conceptions and constraints	1. play involves the intellect 2. as a result of play, the intellect increases in complexity 3. this process in the human can be separated into stages 4. children pass through these stages in order	1. it doesn't account for play when and if the intellect ceases to develop
11. Learning	by the normal processes that produce learning	1. the child acts to increase the probability of pleasant events 2. the child acts to decrease the probability of unpleasant events 3. the environment is a complex of pleasant and unpleasant effects 4. the environment selects and energizes the play behaviors of its tenants	1. it doesn't account for behavior in situations where there are no apparent consequences (However this theory would maintain that there are no such settings.) 2. it doesn't account for the original contributions to behaviors made by an individual's genetic inheritance

MODERN THEORIES
OF PLAY

Chapter 5

In the last decade or so, a series of separate areas of research on behavior have coalesced and provided evidence and theory that explains some behavior in terms of a drive to maintain optimal arousal. The separate research endeavors started about the time of World War II and concerned: the vigilance of human operators; manipulatory, exploratory behaviors in animals; and the effects of sensory and perceptual deprivation on man and animals. The need to maintain optimal arousal has achieved the status of a new drive, and much of the surplus or playful behavior that is enigmatic can now be explained in terms of this drive. In human terms the organism behaves in such a way as to avoid boredom or to avoid unpleasant overstimulation. One set of behaviors serves a stimulus-seeking function and the other as stimulus avoidance.

The major portion of the behavior serving this drive for optimal arousal is concerned with stimulus-seeking, and this behavior, it will be argued, includes play as we presently view it.

The effect of the primary drives and stimulus-avoidance is different from stimulus-seeking. The behavior elicited by the primary drives reduces the intensity of the internal stimulation signaling the need. Conversely, stimulus-seeking behavior tends to increase the level of stimulation, usually derived externally from the organism. This concept avoids a trap into which earlier theories had fallen since it does not assume that the natural state for man and all animals is quiescence, and counters older concepts that the organism only behaved to restore its systems to a quiet state. The "quiescence" idea courses through many of the theories of behavior (see Freeman, 1948; Zipf, 1949, for reviews of these ideas), and the theories of play covered already.

Modern views of behavior are similar to the old views in that behavior is held to be motivated; driven by some thing or some system. However, the process is a dynamic one, at least for the surplus behavior not required for survival. The organism has a need for stimulus-seeking behavior that is only interrupted by the need to eliminate fatigue by sleep and to satisfy prepotent primary drives. The normal state of the organism reflects the state of its nervous system which is in a state of constant activity. The normal organism needs to be in constant receipt of the sensory input from the environment that satisfies its need for stimulation.

This stimulus-seeking behavior may involve activities that apparently have potential for sustaining the organism or may be apparently useless. In the former case the behavior is classified as serious and in the latter case playful. In other words, serious behavior, work, can satisfy two kinds of needs or drives, those associated with drive reduction and those concerned with stimulation, whereas the surplus playful behavior is motivated only by a need for stimulation. Our concern is primarily with stimulus-seeking without prejudicing the notion that work can be playful.

Neophilia and Neophobia

Both views of the natural state of the organism, quiescence and continual stimulus-seeking, seem to have some validity. Some organisms are apparently quiescent when all their drives are satiated. Others, particularly the mammals, seem to fit the view that animals are normally active. Morris (1964) assigns animals to two basic groups, the neophilic and neophobic. He characterizes the neophilic or novelty-liking animals as those with a wide behavioral repertoire living in plastic environmental niches where adaptive responses and up-to-date information about the environment are at a selective premium. He refers to these as the entrepreneurs of the animal kingdom, e.g., rodents, dogs, bears, and primates. On the other hand, neophobic animals are highly specialized, living in rigid niches with small behavioral repertoires, like the reptiles. The question why an animal emits this apparently surplus behavior becomes increasingly important to the extent that the organism under consideration can be characterized as neophilic. The question is a useful one since this treatment is primarily concerned with the nonutilitarian behavior of the most neophilic of animals, man, and since the more neophobic the animal the less nonutilitarian or playful behavior there is to explain.

Morris does not mean that animals can be divided into two groups, but that they lie roughly on a continuum, the poles of which he labeled neophilic and neophobic. Morris' argument becomes circular if the emission of playful behavior is the criterion for the classification, whereby play is defined as the nonutilitarian behavior emitted by neophilic animals.

However, his classification of animals along a continuum corresponds generally to another classification depending on the anatomy of the brain. Hunt (1965) integrates the thinking on the neuroanatomy of the brain and the behavioral complexity of the vertebrates. The brain of a vertebrate seems to have two major areas that Hebb (1966) referred to originally as the association and the sensory-motor areas. The approximate ratio of these areas to which these functions were ascribed he called the A/S ratio. This ratio corresponds to what Hunt (1965) prefers to call the I/E ratio. The I/E ratio relates the portion of the brain concerning neural events that arise internally (intrinsically) to that portion dealing with external or extrinsic neural traffic. They are merely a relabeling of Hebb's association versus sensory-motor ratio.

The importance of the ratio was explained by Hunt (1965):

> The ratio is low in such vertebrates as reptiles and amphibia, where the anatomical provision for semi-autonomous central processes intervening between receptor inputs and motor outputs is highly limited. It increases up through the orders of mammals, reaching its maximum in man [p. 206].

Thus, as the I/E or A/S ratio increases, the rigidity of the behavior exhibited by animals decreases, and the capacity for new behaviors, given similar environmental inputs, increases. Animals with large portions of the brain tissue given over to, presumably, memory and association, can learn and behave adaptively to subtle differences in their environment. As the ratio becomes very large, the major strategy in a species' struggle for survival is that it is not tied to rigid unmodulated responses to given stimulus patterns. Thus, the continuum of vertebrates arranged in ascending order of their A/S ratios would have significant similarity to Morris' organization of vertebrates along the neophobic-neophilic continuum.

The process whereby such a trend in the evolution of vertebrates was generated seems to be straightforward. Species responding to critical changes in their environment by means of a process of Darwinian selection of the fittest could only do so slowly and were presumably often ill-equipped to meet acute challenges to change their modus vivendi. Species that were behaviorally flexible were better able to modify their behavior within the life span of an individual. Thus, in variable situations the exigencies of survival would exert a selective pressure in favor of flexibility. To go further, unpredictable changes would present the greatest challenges, and individuals best suited to the new circumstances behaviorally and morphologically would be at a selective advantage.

Up-to-date information about the multiplicity of elements in the individual's habitat, both currently useful for survival and apparently useless, would be to the advantage of the animal as preparation for future

changes.   Thus, the individual and species living within a varying ecosystem is better prepared to meet its challenges to the extent that it has
explored, manipulated, responded to, or played with the elements or
ones similar to them in its environmental niche before they became critical.   Hence, the incessant activity of the neophilic animals, their consistent curiosity concerning new elements, and their emission of new
responses are integral to the survival of the organism.

It can be argued that the behaviors that are currently nonutilitarian,
although they may have payoff later in that the animal is then individually better able to cope with an alteration, must be sustained at the time
by some reinforcing mechanism (motive).   Probably only a few of the
knowledges or behaviors acquired during nonutilitarian behavior will
prove critical, and the delay between acquisition and payoff will be
highly variable.   In the absence of some intervening mechanism for immediate reinforcement, the surplus behavior that characterizes the neophilic individuals and species would be extinguished.

What may be acquired through play or nonutilitarian behavior is a
general problem-solving set.   By virtue of exposure to problem situations
whose resolutions are not critical, the animal develops a series of strategies for dealing with classes of problems likely to beset it in a particular
habitat.   The possessors of better sets and strategies, which in a continually varying ecosystem means a greater capacity to deal with that unknown variety of forthcoming changes, will tend to be selected for.

Stimulus-seeking viewed in this context must clearly be one of the
determinants of survival.   The question of what intervening mechanisms
elicit this important class of behavior is the point of this chapter.   There
are two closely related explanations which depend on the same intervening mechanism that maintains playful or nonutilitarian behavior.   The
first identifies a drive for new-stimulus events which characterizes play as
stimulus-seeking behavior.   The other claims that the nonutilitarian behavior of the animal is maintained by a need to produce effects on the
environment to demonstrate competence and is White's (1959) concept
of competence/effectance motivation.

Play as Stimulus-Seeking : History of the Idea

As usual the central concepts for a theory did not burst onto the scene
ready for instant assembly.   The idea of stimulus-seeking has had a long
history.   The notion first appears in Pavlov's (1927) description of the
investigatory or orienting reflex.

> It is this reflex which brings about the immediate response in man and
> animals to the slightest changes in the world around them, so that they

immediately orientate their appropriate receptor organ in accordance with
the perceptible quality in the agent bringing about the change, making full
investigation of it. The biological significance of this reflex is obvious.
If the animal were not provided with such a reflex its life would hang
at every moment by a thread. In man this reflex has been greatly developed with far-reaching results, being represented in its highest form by
inquisitiveness—the parent of that scientific method through which we
hope one day to come to a true orientation in knowledge of the world
around us [Pavlov, 1927, p. 12].

The occurrence of a detectable change in the stimulus environment
gives rise to the orienting reflex which is described in great detail by
Berlyne (1960). The changes are many, rippling out through a great
variety of physiological mechanisms. They function generally to mobi-
lize the animal for swift execution of an appropriate response. Current
responses are stopped till sufficient information is received concerning
the new event to decide which action is appropriate. The orienting reflex to a particular stimulus can be extinguished by its repeated presentation and providing the stimulus does not signal some other impending
critical event, the animal soon ceases to be startled by it as it becomes
familiar. It has been recognized then for many years that an animal is
capable of selective attention. Only the new stimulus events or those
tied to another and important event are the subject of the investigatory
reflex. The multiplicity of familiar and expected stimulus events are
not attended to.

The issue is simply one of selective attention. How does the animal
sort from the panoply of stimulus events occurring at any given time those
in which there has been a change? The animal must form expectations
as a result of experience against which the current stimulus events are
continuously compared (Miller, Galanter & Pribram, 1960). Lack of con-
gruity between the current expectation and a stimulus event is signalled
and attention given it. The process of monitoring the sensory input
must occur automatically since only when an incongruity occurs are the
activities of highest conscious centers interrupted. Despite the obvious
importance for survival, the mere selection of startling events for attention does not explain the deliberate seeking of new stimulus inputs or
alterations in the current stimuli that characterizes neophilic animals.
This issue was addressed long ago by McDougall (1923).

McDougall concluded that there was an instinct of curiosity which was
not directed towards any particular activity or object. Its function was
simply to prepare the animal for the exercise of a more specific instinct
by collecting information.

The object (using this word again in the widest way to include every kind
of perceptible situation) that is to excite curiosity must have some degree

of resemblance to objects that normally evoke some other instinct, or it will fail to draw the attention of the animal; but, under the particular conditions of the moment, it must present so much of a novelty, or of the unusual as not to excite that other instinct or fail to excite it in full strength [McDougall, 1923, p. 143].

McDougall understood that selective attention depended upon an incongruity between expectation and actuality, knew that it was important for survival, and that higher vertebrates often deliberately engaged in exploratory activity. However, he had no way to explain this behavior. In the context of the times he simply argued that there must be an instinct to drive the behavior.

Recent Research Thrusts

After the era of the instinct there followed World War II and the era of the grand learning theories of psychology in the forties. This period was largely concerned with the psychology of need reduction. However, it was during this period that three major lines of research were in an empirical phase, marshalling data for a theoretical leap that occurred in the late fifties and sixties. These endeavors, research on human vigilance, sensory deprivation, and the manipulative-exploratory behavior of primates, all apparently widely separated, eventually all contributed to the body of theory concerning arousal and arousal-seeking behavior.

"Vigilance research concerns the attentiveness of the subject and his capability for detecting changes in stimulus events over relatively long periods of sustained observation [Frankmann & Adams, 1962, p. 259]." The early research on vigilance was stimulated by the application of technology to watch keeping. Radar, sonar, and asdic all required the detection of transient and infrequent signals occurring during long watches. The operators' task was merely to decide whether a signal was present and to signal a detection, and yet they could not seem to maintain their critical level of performance.

The first important paper on this topic (Mackworth, 1950) used a simple clock test where the subject had to detect occasional double jumps of the sweep second hand. Mackworth reported a startling decrease in detection rate over a two-hour watch. In a series of studies aimed at finding why this decrement occurred, Mackworth noted that a short telephone call to check whether the S was all right restored performance. Why the decrement in the first place? Why the restoration of performance? Much research was initiated and data was collected on the nature, frequency, and predictability of the signal, and its mode of presentation. This work is reviewed in Frankmann and Adams (1962), Buckner and McGrath (1963), and Mackworth (1970).

During this early concern with variables influencing the detection of simple signals, technology became more complex. The problem shifted to a concern with the detection of rare events in highly complex displays such as those required for air traffic control. It was noted that in highly complex situations the detection rate did not diminish over time as it did in the simple detection situations. Although the time taken to respond increased during the watch, the necessity to integrate signals from the complex displays and make decisions seemed to maintain detection performance (Kibler, 1965).

Several theories were advanced to account for the data which have since been integrated to form a rather complicated theory (Mackworth, 1970). The theory takes into account the difficulty in deciding whether a signal occurred or not, the predictability of the signal, and the arousal level of the operator. On the way to this complex but more complete formulation, an arousal theory was advanced in isolation (Frankmann & Adams, 1962) and exemplified the implication of arousal theory in explaining another area of behavior.

To concentrate on the operator's arousal, rather than the other aspects, the influence of the afferent stimuli on the reticulate arousal system in the brain was implicated. The theory stated that the afferent stimuli are carried along two paths in the brain. One path carries information to the higher brain, and the other modifies the state of arousal of the individual by triggering the reticulate system. Complex, incongruous, or novel stimuli lead to arousal. In the absence of arousing action the subject becomes progressively less alert, detecting fewer signals, unless a surprising or arousing stimulus arouses him for a time. It was discovered that the arousal of the individual could be maintained in a variety of ways by adding signals or extraneous events, or by increasing the signal complexity and predictability. Subjects were also reported to be deliberately generating stimulus input by fidgeting, daydreaming, or other self-stimulations.

The concept of arousal being maintained by the input of novel, surprising, or complex stimuli was strengthened by the work in another area of behavior, vigilance, that was originally undertaken for the pragmatic reason of maintaining the performance of human operators during boring vigils.

During this time and along another line of research there started a series of studies on the effect of depriving men of stimuli. Hebb (1966) had already postulated that the natural state of the nervous system was not quiescence, and depriving it of sensory stimuli of any kind was required to test his theories. From this has developed an extensive body of studies concerning man's intolerance for massive reductions of stimulus input. The basic paradigm was to reduce the quantity of stimulation reaching the subject for a long period of time and observe the effects on the subject's physiological functioning; his performance of given tasks, susceptibility to change in attitudes, general behavior, changes in diurnal rhythms, and his self-reports of the experience.

The early studies went to great lengths to deprive the subjects of stimuli generated by the environment and those generated by the subject. They were suspended weightless in turbulence-free water at skin temperature in a soundproof tank and told to hang passively. The early reports were alarming. Although the self-reports showed that after an initial sleep the experience was aversive, several subjects maintained their deprivation until they hallucinated. Afterwards their behavior was disturbed in a variety of ways, sometimes for several weeks (Zubek, 1964).

Later experiments did not replicate the early hallucinations, presumably because of the publicity or because the experience was perceived as less dangerous because others had survived, but the research proceeded to amass data. A crucial finding was that the existence of stimuli themselves was not sufficient to eliminate the aversive effects of the experimental settings. The emission of similar quantities of stimulus energy as would be emitted in a normal setting was not sufficient to stave off the effects of deprivation. The crucial factor seemed to be presence of meaningful patterns in the stimuli. A hissing or white noise may generate the same quantum of energy in the ears, but the subject cannot generate from it patterns of input that can be attended to. The elimination of form, pattern, or meaning from the input to the subject results in perceptual deprivation, as distinguished from the elimination of all stimuli or sensory deprivation.

The most recent theorizing concerning the effects of sensory and perceptual deprivation invoke a concept of optimal stimulation and are reviewed carefully by Jones (1969), Zuckerman (1969), and Suedfeld (1969). The major points made are that there is a clear need for stimulus input that contains patterns or information and that these inputs, depending on a variety of other variables, change the state of the subject. The state is one of arousal and the effects are seen as being mediated in the nervous system, presumably by the reticulate arousal system.

While research on sensory deprivation and vigilance proceeded, work was already underway on a class of behaviors exhibited by animals that was puzzling in the context of the need-reduction theories of motivation that were then extant. Two classes of behaviors seemed to be emitted without the necessity of an extrinsic reward. Monkeys were shown to possess a tendency to manipulate elements in the environment and rats to explore new situations independently of any reward being contingent on the behavior.

Monkeys have been shown to persist in manipulating gadgets that resemble puzzles (Harlow, Harlow & Meyer, 1950; Harlow, 1950) even though they were never associated with rewards. The animals seemed to be motivated merely by the existence of the puzzle itself and persisted in the behavior. Two explanations were advanced. Harlow (1953) added a new drive to account for the behavior by asserting that it was motivated by a manipulatory drive. The other, a more general concept, was advanced by Nissen (1954) who claimed that the ability to emit a response was its own motivation. This suggested that the very existence of a response in the repertoire carried with it a need for its exercise. Thus, all behaviors can be assumed to be emitted at some time just because the mechanisms for their emission exist. Other expressions of this concept appear in Woodworth's behavior primacy (1958) model and in White's effectance motivation which will be dealt with later in the chapter.

Nissen (1930) showed that rats would cross an electrified grid in order to earn the opportunity to explore what lay on the other side. By 1953, Montgomery had shown the rats would explore whether satiated or not, that the opportunity to explore a complex maze was reinforcing (1954). Harlow (1953) noted that rats would choose to go the long way around a maze on their way to their reward, presumably because of the intrinsic rewards associated with the more complex experience. Butler (1953) showed that monkeys would learn discrimination problems for a reward which was merely the opportunity to look at the normal activities of the laboratory around the cage. There are many, many examples similar to these. They have been reviewed by Butler (1958a and b), Cofer (1959), and Welker (1961).

This enigmatic behavior was presumed to be motivated and the problem was solved by formulating a new drive—a drive for exploration.

The research to date and the various theoretical notions that derive from these researches on manipulation and exploration were integrated definitively by Berlyne, first in his book *Conflict, Arousal and Curiosity* (1960), and then in several articles (Berlyne, 1963, 1966, 1968). The essential feature of his integration was his connection of these behaviors not to a collection of named motives, but to a theoretical formulation that had its base in one mechanism. This led to a more precise formulation of what was happening inside the animal while it was emitting the apparently surplus behaviors. Berlyne's integration implicated the reticulate system again.

Although the three areas of research briefly touched on have not been formally integrated, the theory of behavior advanced by Berlyne and others could bring about such integration. These theories of behavior owed much to these lines of thinking, and to the neurophysiologists who discovered the reticulate arousal system. The insights they provide into a subclass of behaviors that are not apparently motivated by the traditional need reduction models are powerful indeed.

The Neural Mechanisms of Arousal

Arousal or activation is the subject of voluminous writings. Hinde (1966) reviews the extensive work so far undertaken on the arousal mechanisms in the brain and Duffy (1957), Samuels (1959), and Berlyne (1960) have surveyed the physiological concomitants of arousal. The evidence clearly implicates the reticulate arousal system as the mediating mechanism responsible for the process of arousal. The RAS is a diffuse network in the lower brain contiguous with both the afferent pathway carrying sensory input from the body and outside to the cortex and the efferent pathways descending from the brain to the peripheral nervous system. It receives collateral fibres from the sensory tracts and provides indirect routes to the higher brain for incoming stimulation by means of multitudinous connections with the cerebral cortex. The cortex and the reticulate arousal system (RAS) are intimately connected and stand on opposite sides of a balance with the RAS exerting an arousing influence on the body system generally and the cortex inhibiting the RAS. The resultant effect determines the level of arousal of the animal.

When the RAS is injured or anesthetized the organism subsides into somnolence, whereas if it is excited the organism becomes overtly alert. Stimulus input can cause the disinhibition of the RAS by the cortex in proportion to its "impact." Impact was defined by Fiske and Maddi (1961) in terms of its intensity, its meaningfulness, and also the extent to which it differs from preceding stimulation. If the stimulus is intense, is associated with some critical event, or is in some way novel, unexpected, or incongruous, then the cortex is unable to prepare an adequate inhibition to counter the effect generated by the arrival of the same stimulus input in the RAS. The imbalance in favor of the RAS creates an increase in the arousal level of the organism until the intense or unusual event has been habituated to, reacted to, or recategorized as innocuous.

Increasing the general activation or arousal of the animal results first in an increase in performance, up to some optimal level, after which further increases in arousal reduce performance. The inverted "U" function expresses the idea that it is possible to be so aroused that performance suffers, presumably because the responding is in some way disorganized (Figure 5.1).

If the cortex is given time to organize for inhibition of the RAS it can be kept in its place. For example, if the stimulus intensity is altered gradually no arousal takes place, but if it is suddenly altered to the same

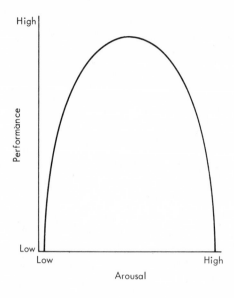

High

Performance

Low

Low   High

Arousal

Figure 5.1
The inverted "U" function relating
performance to arousal.

level the animal is aroused. Also, if the animal can anticipate a normally surprising or arousing stimulus event then the arousal level is reduced or occurs gradually so that there is less disorganization of the performance.

The system works selectively, the cortex acting back on the RAS to inhibit arousal if the stimulus input is repetitious, expected, innocuous, irrelevant, redundant, etc.

The cortex, however, may also act on the RAS to cause it to arouse the animal. Presumably this action results when cognitive events have occurred that have salience for the animal. In human terms, it occurs after thinking some new or important combination of old experiences or associations has taken place. The animal in this case has generated from the residual products of past experience events within the brain capable of self-activation. So when novel or unexpected input from outside, novel cognitive combinations or thoughts about previous experiences, or novel interactions between cognitive events and stimulus events occur, the cortical inhibition is removed and the RAS is allowed to arouse the organism.

The processes involved are dynamic. The degree of arousal varies extensively with variations in balance existing in the interplay between the cortex and RAS. This balance is in turn dependent on the ongoing cognitive and sensory events working on the system.

Higher animals, with their broader response repertoire, are capable of self-arousal. They can disturb both the sensory input on the one hand, and can generate cognitive events that are arousing on the other. They also can act to reduce their exposure to arousing events. These capabilities and their utilization allow the maintenance of an optimal arousal level for an individual. This was first expressed by Hebb and Thompson (1954) who stated that organisms tend to act so as to produce an optimal level of excitation. Organisms tend to emit responses that have as a result a change in the arousal level towards the optimum. Deviations from the optimal level become increasingly aversive and the individual acts to diminish the aversiveness. This view is supported cogently by Leuba (1955), Berlyne (1960), Fiske and Maddi (1961), and Hinde (1966).

States of arousal that are not optimal result in responses by the animal to rectify the situation. An animal that is sub-optimally aroused, and that does not need sleep, attempts to generate interactions with the environment which will produce sensory or cognitive input to the cortex that will lead to disinhibition of the RAS and an elevation of arousal level.

Stimulus Events and Impact

Under these circumstances the behaviors emitted by an animal are those most likely to produce sensory or cognitive stimulus events that have impact or potential for being selected from the ongoing but familiar events in which they are embedded. The animal behaves to generate stimulus events which have the attributes that make for selective attention. Berlyne (1960) has classified these attributes. The stimulus must have some degree of novelty, uncertainty or dissonance, or complexity.

Novelty can mean that the event is completely novel in that it has never been experienced before, or novel in the sense that it has not been experienced recently. In another sense it can be absolutely novel in that none of the attributes of the stimulus input have been experienced before, or can be relatively novel in that only some of the attributes are different.

The problem of relative novelty is important. The incoming stimuli are likely to be categorized according to a concept of best fit. For example, perceiving a piece of furniture, a "table," involves the integration of the input with preceding inputs concerning the categorization of the context and the pattern of stimulus events. Thus, the patterns of light, shade, and color, plus the fact that the object stands in a space already categorized as a "room," for example, leads to its classification as a table. However, attention continues to be given selectively to the attributes that are unlike the common attributes of all "tables." After many tables have been seen it will be difficult to find one that has considerable novelty relative to the others and still have it function as a "table." Looking at "tables" soon ceases to be arousing.

Intermediate novelty seems to be preferred. Complete or absolute novelty poses problems in that there are no extant categories against which the new experience can be compared. The absolutely novel experience presumably carries an aversively high arousal potential.

Dissonance may be created by building an expectation by previous exposures, and then introducing a change in sequence so that the next event is unexpected. This can be done by varying the pattern or intensity of the stimuli, the modality through which the signal comes, or by altering its timing. These alterations generate uncertainty as to what the outcome of a situation will be. Thus, if a response (R) always leads to the same stimulus (S), the probability of $R \to S$ is 1. Once an $R \to S$ relation becomes completely predictable it has no uncertainty and the result, S, can never be novel. It can have no arousal potential or impact.

Uncertainty is resolved by the outcome and the outcome carries information. If R can lead to two equally probable outcomes, S1 and S2, then the respondent is maximally uncertain as to which is likely to result. Responding to see which one occurs, S1 or S2, reduces the uncertainty and produces information. In this case information theory states that 1 BIT of information has passed. Had there been not two but four possibilities, 2 BITS of information would pass, and with eight possibilities 3 BITS of information, and so on. So one BIT, or binary digit, represents the information in one simple choice. Turning the case around, it is possible that a stimulus, S, can elicit two responses, R1 and R2. If the links between the two responses and the stimulus are equally strong, there is maximal conflict between the responses and there is uncertainty as to which one will be emitted. This is the case of maximal choice. It is possible to continue this argument about how much information passes when the different outcomes are not equally probable (see Berlyne, 1960; Edwards, 1969; Cherry, 1966; Attneave, 1959), but the important issue is that when uncertainty is resolved then information passes.

A further way to manipulate the impact of a stimulus event is to modify its complexity. Increasing the complexity of an event, object, or situation is achieved by increasing the number of distinguishable components, by increasing the dissimilarity of the components, and by manipulating the elements so that they cannot be categorized as just one item reacted to simply. Thus, with more complex situations there are more interrelations between events and components that are possible. The more possible combinations or outcomes, the greater the potential for uncertainty or the greater the information load the event or object has.

The elements of novelty, complexity, and the conflict between likely outcomes are all closely related. They have in common the fact that the animal's predictions of the outcome are not completely reliable. There is uncertainty. The information load in the event or interaction seems to be the essential quality that is arousing. Certainties are not normally selected for attention. Some intermediate level of information flow is optimally arousing, and too much uncertainty is supra-optimally arousing and leads to disorganization if escape is prevented.

A New Drive for Optimal Arousal

The notions that an optimal arousal level exists and that information flow is arousing were explicitly combined by Schultz (1965) into a new drive for processing information to maintain optimal arousal. He called the process *sensoristasis*, a process analogous to homeostasis, whereby the animal maintains an informational or "sensory" *milieu internale* in the same way that physiological mechanisms keep the various tissues within a tolerable range of their optimal conditions.

> Sensoristasis can be defined as a drive state of critical arousal which impels the organism (in a waking state) to strive to maintain an optimal level of sensory variation. There is, in other words, a drive to maintain a constant range of varied sensory input in order to maintain cortical arousal at an optimum level [Schultz, 1965, p. 30].

Schultz argues that the sensoristatic model fits the three logically distinct characteristics of a drive in that it is an energizing condition affecting activity level, it selectively alters the likelihood of responses occurring, and its alleviation is rewarding. This new drive takes its place with other drives in energizing and selecting behavior. Thus, in circumstances where primary or visceral drives are satisfied, behavior is maintained by the sensoristatic drive state. The animal continues to seek for a varied sensory input—the fodder of the drive for optimal arousal.

Schultz's formulation is built on a drive reductionist's view of behavior which claims that behavior that results in a reward is learned. That which is not rewarded or reinforced drops out of the repertoire. The drive, which is assumed to be mediated by some mechanism, as a result energizes and selects the response to be emitted. The stronger the drive, the stronger the tendency to emit the response. The drive state is usually conceived of as the accumulation of some need that at first increasingly pressures the animal to satisfy that need. The animal becomes aroused or restless, indulges in generalized seeking or appetitive behavior and continues to do so until it comes across an opportunity to emit the response that satisfies the need, the consummatory act. The act is accompanied by the reduction of the need or drive and positive affect or pleasure (Lindsley, 1964). The stress resulting from an unsatisfied need continues to build to the point where the organism is disorganized or weakened and then the behavior emitted ceases to be adaptive.

The reduction of the drive presumably is pleasant and the behavior that leads to it is reinforced. The animal learns which responses are reinforced positively and which responses will lead to a heightened drive state which is aversive. The animal tends to avoid making those responses which are aversive and vice versa. The sensoristatic or stimulus-seeking model works in exactly that way. When the primary drives are satisfied the animal continues to emit stimulus-seeking behavior in response to the sensoristatic drive. The animal learns to maintain an optimal level of arousal (Figure 5.2).

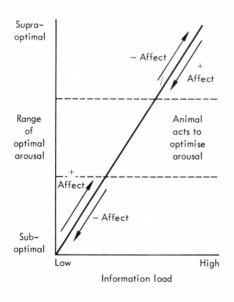

Figure 5.2
The relationship between information load and arousal accounts for the behavior of the animal as it acts to optimize level of arousal.

The theory explains which behavior is emitted when the primary drives are satisfied, and why the animal seeks to increase stimulation rather than eliminate it. However, the constraints of the cortico-reticular system decree that any stimulus will not suffice for the elevation of optimal arousal. The stimuli must have impact or arousing potential. It is not sufficient for the animal seeking optimal arousal merely to be exposed to stimuli. The stimuli must in some way reduce uncertainty or carry information. Therefore, the animal strives to optimize its exposure to situations and events that contain appropriate levels of novelty, or conflict or complexity. The theory also explains why quiescence is not the normal state, at least in the higher vertebrates having cortico-reticular systems to provide the drive and high A/S ratios to allow the generation of variable responses.

At this point it is important to recognize that the preceding discussion has fallen naturally into the assumption that the animal is sub-optimally aroused and is striving to elevate its arousal level towards the optimum. Inherent in the sensoristatic model is the possibility that the animal is supra-optimally aroused. In this case the animal learns to behave to diminish its arousal level (see Figure 5.2).

However, for the purposes of simplicity in the discussion the needs for increasing and decreasing arousal and their opposite strategies will be separated. For the ensuing discussion it will be assumed that the animal is sub-optimally aroused and is under pressure from the sensoristatic drive to increase the arousal level.

That sub-optimal arousal is the more frequent occurrence is neatly explained by the nature of the animal and the nature of the environment. During its life-span the animal has an ongoing need to process information, yet a particular environment has a relatively limited quantity of information. The limit is determined by the capacities for interaction possessed by the animal and its complexity. As the effects of previous interactions with the environment accumulate, the greater the probability that the immediate stimulus event is familiar and will be reacted to as a simple entity, if at all. With the accumulation of experience the cognitive structure of the animal itself becomes more complex, and requires more complex events to maintain the passage of information. Dember and Earl (1957) and Sackett (1965) recognized this and added a rider, that will by now seem obvious: an animal has a limited capacity for uncertainty. An animal of given complexity can only cope with complexities and uncertainties in the environment that produce an information load within its current processing ability.

They went on to make explicit the concept of an optimal disparity between the current complexity of the animal on the one hand and the complexity of its interactions with the environment on the other. They labelled those stimulus events that contribute to the struggle for optimal arousal as "pacers." To use an example from Dember and Earl's paper:

> Some stimuli may be too complex to act as pacers. A person just learning French will not improve on being exposed to Proust or Baudelaire, though he may be able to evaluate their work as much more complex than that in his elementary text [Dember and Earl, 1957, p. 95].

"Pacers" generate optimally arousing information loads and advance the animal upward along a scale of complexity (Figure 5.2). Clearly then the content of the interactions with the environment cannot remain static. If the animal is to maintain an information flow it must ever contain new elements of increasing complexity.

What is new or arousing can only be defined in terms of the preceding experiences of the individual organism. So the level of complexity of the organism and what is arousing are dependent on the phenotype. Today's arousing interactions are part of the stream of interactions between inheritance and experience.

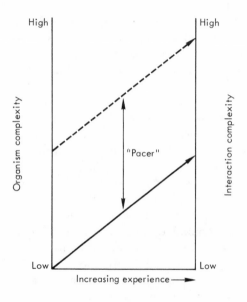

Figure 5.3
Sackett's (1965) pacer concept showing the maintenance of an optimal disparity between organismic and environmental complexity over time.

Waddington (1968) clarified thinking on biological phenomena like the pacer concept described above when he coined a new word—*homeorhesis*. He defined homeorhesis as a property exhibited by ". . . a system (that) exhibits a tendency towards a certain kind of equilibrium which is restored after a disturbance; but this equilibrium is not centered on a static state, but rather on a direction or pathway of change [p. 32]." As Schultz's term sensoristasis is derived directly from Cannon's (1932) term homeostasis, it should perhaps be modified to indicate clearly the changing nature of the interactions necessary for optimal arousal. The direction or pathway of change is clearly toward one of increasing complexity of interaction with the accumulation of experience. The static element implied by the suffix *-stasis* applies only to the concept of optimal arousal, not to the stimulus events leading to it.

Arousal-Seeking Behaviors

For the maintenance of optimal arousal the animal requires the opportunity to produce interactions with the environment that carry arousal potential. The sensoristatic drive reinforces those responses which lead to optimal arousal so that in an appropriate environment the animal learns to maintain arousal within the optimal range. This leads directly to the question, "What behaviors do animals characteristically employ to generate the kind of stimulation that elevates their arousal towards an optimum?" Once more Berlyne (1960) provides the initial lead in proposing a categorization and reviewing much of the research done.

At the simplest level an animal situated among optimally arousing stimuli does nothing but selectively attend to various arousing stimuli as they arrive. The mechanism is simply an orientational one involving what Pavlov earlier described as the orienting or investigatory reflex. If the stimulus calls for no other reaction and is repeated, it soon loses its arousal potential.

If an object is placed in the situation which is sufficiently novel so that previous experiences are not sufficient to provide reliable estimates of what is likely to happen, then it will engender a conflict. The stimuli it produces will lead to the possibility of two responses—to avoid the object to avoid the possibility that it may be noxious in some unknown way, and to approach to reduce the uncertainties that it holds and generate information. The conflict is resolved by a gradual process in which the various attributes of the novel object are tested.

The procedure that commonly occurs is for the animal to first indulge in locomotor exploration. Investigating the situation by moving around the object allows the exploration of its properties by distance receptors, while preserving the options for escape. Repetition of the visual and auditory and olfactory exploration of the stimulus situation, providing the object or situation does not emit an unexpected stimulus to startle the explorer, will reduce the arousal and conflict and the animal then moves closer and eventually on to the next phase.

This initial approach/avoidance conflict is resolved progressively more rapidly as the novelty wears off (Linford & Jeanrenaud, 1970). That the time taken to approach the novel object diminishes with repeated exposures has been shown in two simple studies by Jeanrenaud (1969) and Lovelace (1971).

Berlyne (1960) differentiates two aspects of exploration. The responses emitted by an animal that is seeking information about a specific object or situation are called specific exploration. However, when the animal is in a state of sub-optimal arousal and responds to that need by seeking nonspecifically for some source of arousing stimuli, then it is indulging in diversive exploration.

Locomotor exploration does not involve interaction with the object or situation but when sufficient exploration by the distance receptors has been done so that approach/avoidance conflicts are resolved, the animal begins to employ the peripheral sensors to gain more information. It begins to investigate. Investigation is a process whereby the animal tests the object, employing the peripheral sensors to determine the contingencies associated with it. The animal investigates the outcomes of its interactions with the object or situation. The object is repeatedly felt, sniffed, tasted, hefted, shoved, pulled, turned, etc., and its various components are treated similarly. The situation is different from the approach/avoidance conflict where one source of stimuli produced two competing tendencies to respond. At this stage in the process there is uncertainty as to what will be the outcome or stimuli resulting from an investigatory or manipulatory response. Here, the information is carried by the possibilities for different stimuli being produced by one response.

If the object is simple and relatively familiar, very soon reliable predictions can be made about what will happen after a given response by the animal. When the outcome is highly predictable there is little uncertainty and the arousal potential diminishes. If the object or situation is complex (has many distinguishably dissimilar elements and cannot be reacted to as a whole), then the process of reducing the uncertainty concerning the relations between the responses applied to the object and the outcome may take many repetitions. Where it is not possible to make completely reliable connections, it is possible for the process of exploration to go on indefinitely.

It is usual, however, for an object to cease to be attended to either because the uncertainties connected with it have been reduced, or a more attractive or arousing system is in competition with it. However, as time elapses between exposures, the object's arousal potential is to some extent restored as familiarity is reduced. In other words, the certainty that the old and reliable connections between the animal's response and the outcome is reduced because they have been to some extent forgotten or because the animal may hypothesize that the properties of the object may have changed since the last exposure. The object is then reinvestigated to determine whether the old and remembered predictions still hold and to explore for new outcomes.

Social animals also use the existence of others to develop arousing stimulation. Animals often systematically emit signals or responses directed at another animal of the same or other species (Hebb & Thompson, 1954) in order to observe the response generated in them. The ebb and flow of such social interaction is filled with information. The range of such activities from rough-and-tumble play of young animals through the interplay of after-dinner conversation is characterized by the deliberate creation of uncertainty. "How will the other animal react to that?" and "How will I manage the reaction?" epitomize the playful thrusts and parries of much of social interaction that is not bound to the achievement of some critical goal.

Epistemic Behavior

Humans, at least, are also capable of maintaining arousal by the maniplation of symbolic experiences. The rearrangement of old ideas, or the process of fitting new ideas into existing frameworks carries with it uncertainty. The higher processes of thesis, antithesis, and synthesis are activities that are fraught with uncertainty and can be arousing. Reading novels or newspapers, daydreaming, problem-solving are all activities actively sought after by humans, particularly by adults who by virtue of their age have a richer lode of experiences to mine. The exercise of the higher processes, in the absence of any overt response, may be arousing and the provision of the wherewithal for this activity forms the major component of the entertainment and communications industry (Stephenson, 1967).

Berlyne (1960) deals with the question of the arousal potential of human cognitive events. Conflicts between ideas resulting from past experience or lack of information necessary to resolve such a conflict feature largely in the mental activities of man. Thinking involves the ongoing process of classifying and ordering ideas into parsimonious systems to explain and predict events in the environment. Mismatch or dissonance between segments of these mental systems creates conflict which is arousing in its own right. The reconciliation of inconsistencies requires reordering, redefining, and usually additional information. The process of resolving these conflicts Berlyne calls epistemic behavior (Berlyne, 1960, 1966; Burgers, 1966). His term, from the Greek *episteme* for knowledge, characterizes the motive for much human behavior as knowledge-seeking.

There is simple equivalence between the motives for stimulus-seeking and knowledge-seeking behavior. Stimulus-seeking behavior means more than merely seeking exposure to any stimuli. The stimuli must have arousal potential. They must be to some extent novel or not congruent with established systems. They must contain information in the sense that their perception reduces uncertainty. Knowledge-seeking or epistemic behavior has the same characteristics in that it results in the reduction of conflicts, mismatches, and uncertainties. They share the same motive. The confusing element is merely that the stimulus-seeking behavior of adult humans may not result in any overt behavior since the interplay of stimulus-events can be entirely cognitive, whereas in the young the interactions are more often between cognitive events and physical events. As the properties of the immediate environment become known, the adult human retreats into his brain or indulges in more sophisticated explorations of the environment not normally classified as play. Closely associated with the processes of epistemic behavior are laughter and humor. Berlyne's recent thorough review of laughter, humor, and play (1968) shows that humor, and its overt behavioral concomitants smiling and laughter, are created by variables such as novelty, surprise, incongruity, ambiguity, complexity, all of which possess arousal potential. Humor is a cognitive process whereby a sequence of stimuli or ideas are strung together in such a way as to generate an expectation which is shattered or a conflict which is suddenly resolved surprisingly. The resolution of the situation is usually achieved in a manner whereby the outcome is obviously trivial rather than critical. Although laughter may be generated by other events, tickling, relief, nitrous oxide, etc., it is customarily associated with a positive or pleasant affect. That subclass of stimulus-seeking behaviors that are humorous and engender smiles and laughter is generally referred to as fun, and explains the frequent occurrence of the words fun, positive affect, and pleasure in definitions of the word play. The processes of generating fun are the processes of generating and reducing uncertainty in noncritical areas of interaction. Fun has arousal potential.

Play and the Competence/Effectance Motive

At this point another theoretician and his arguments must be considered. The formulation of play as arousal-seeking behavior seems to explain much of the data on and our experience of the variety of behaviors that seem to comprise play. However, the content of play as defined so far leaves one type of behavior to be accounted for. It does not account for satisfactorily the repetitious but unstereotyped behavior that persists after novelty has worn off. This behavior can be described as manipulative and produces effects on the environment. A new motive is advanced by White (1959) to account for this behavior. Briefly, he claims that the behavior is motivated by a need to demonstrate a capacity to control or produce effects in the environment. He called this competence/effectance motivation.

A review and digest of his introductory arguments serves to summarize the points already made concerning play as arousal-seeking, while setting the scene for his proposals for a new motive to explain the same behavior.

White, in advancing his theory of competence motivation, presented a tightly knit argument concerning the unacceptability of exploration as a drive in its own right. He notes that the conventional drives are visceral in origin and come into play when there is a deficit in the tissues outside the nervous system. This promotes activity which is stopped by the consummatory act which eliminates the deficit. Learning results from this such that the animal progressively increases the efficiency with which it meets its needs. This is the conventional drive reduction model that leads to the assumption of quiescence. He points out that exploration does not fit this model and therefore should not be relegated to the status of a primary drive.

Exploration, and presumably its relatives, investigation, manipulation, and epistemic behavior, cannot be connected to a visceral need. The pattern of immediate restoration of exploratory behavior by exposure to novel stimuli suggests that when exploration ceases, it is not exploration itself that is satiated, but only that the old object ceased to elicit the behavior. White decides that the fundamental difference here is that the origin for the behavior is not in the viscera and tissues outside the central nervous system (CNS) but in the nervous system. The state of the CNS interacts with the attributes of the environment to generate the motivated behavior—exploration, etc. The existence of novel elements elicits exploration, which in the final analysis does not produce a final need-reducing consummatory act.

White argues that general activity, exploration, investigation, and manipulation be considered together. By adding epistemic behavior or problem-solving to White's list, we arrive at what have been identified as the separate ingredients comprising play. The collective motive sustaining these behaviors is the resultant elevation of arousal mediated by the reticulate system in the brain.

After this summary White reviews several papers in which the only acceptable conclusion to be reached is that arousal-seeking does not explain all the neurogenic, or nonprimary and secondary drive-reducing behavior. He asks why under some circumstances an animal will continue to emit behavior even though novelty could be presumed to have worn off. For example he cites Kagan and Berkun (1954), who found that the opportunity to run in an activity wheel was a sufficient reinforcement to create learning in rats. The experience contained no novelty and there was apparently no consummatory act. In White's words, "they seemed to want to run." This seems amenable to a surplus energy explanation, particularly since the rats were deprived of activity. However, he goes on to cite two monkey studies (Harlow, 1953; Harlow, Harlow & Meyer, 1950) which showed that rhesus monkeys continued to solve manipulation puzzles that led to no reward. White explains this kind of manipulative behavior with familiar objects as a response to a new motivation which has as its goal the production of effects in the environment.

Taking earlier formulations stemming from psychoanalytic theories, he postulates that these are manifestations of an urge to master the environment. Hendrick (1942) described this as "an inborn drive to do and to learn how to do" and this formulation is similar to Groos's (1898) concept of "joy in being the cause." In Groos's statement the "joy" is presumably the positive affect accompanying successful mastery of an element in the environment.

To define this element of mastery, White writes:

> To give the concept a name I have chosen the word *competence,* which is intended in a broad biological sense rather than in its narrow everyday meaning. As used here, competence will refer to an organism's capacity to interact effectively with its environment. In organisms capable of but little learning, this capacity might be considered an innate attribute, but in the mammals and especially man, with their highly plastic nervous system, fitness to interact with the environment is slowly attained through prolonged feats of learning. In view of the directedness and persistence of the behavior that leads to these feats of learning, I consider it necessary to treat competence as having a motivational aspect, and my central argument will be that the motivation needed to attain competence cannot be wholly derived from sources of energy currently conceptualized as drives or instincts. We need a different kind of motivational idea to account fully for the fact that man and the higher mammals develop a competence in dealing with the environment which they certainly do not have at birth and certainly do not arrive at simply through maturation. Such an idea, I believe, is essential for any biologically sound view of human nature [White, 1956, p. 297].

To the concept of competence, implying ability, White added that the reinforcement associated with mastery or demonstrating competence in maintaining interactions with the environment, was a feeling of efficacy. This would correspond presumably to a feeling of being in control and is the motive sustaining the attempts to achieve competence. He called this effectance and together the ideas comprise White's competence/effectance theory of motivation. Competence results from interactions with the world motivated by effectance.

The result of this is that the child is continually and actively involved in the process of interacting with the surroundings. The motive for this, claims White, lies not in an immediate outcome of the interactions such as increased arousal, improvements in the cognitive schemata, the expenditure of energy, etc., but lies in all of them. "The child appears to be occupied with the agreeable task of developing an effective familiarity with his environment [1959, p. 321]."

The crucial question lies in whether White has really added anything to the arousal-seeking model. The difficulty he addresses seems to be that the arousal-seeking model is presumed to fail to deal with repetitious behavior, and effectance motivation adds the ingredient necessary to account for it. However, the arousal-seeking model can account for repetitious behavior in the following way.

The animal is motivated to generate arousing interactions with the environment. The particular kinds of interactions that generate this elevation of arousal are those that produce information flow. Information is defined as the reduction of uncertainty and the uncertainty derives from the animal's inability to predict accurately an outcome given the antecedent conditions. As more and more interactions are experienced, more and more connections between antecedent-subsequent events are made. More cause-effect relations are established.

Many such cause-effect relations are demonstrated or connected for the young animal merely by observation, without its intervention in the stream of events. However, since the animal is also capable of producing effects on the environment the outcomes of its own responses are subject to the same scrutiny. The establishment of cause-effect relations involving the animal itself as well as the environment at large result in the reduction of uncertainty or the flow of information and the elevation of arousal.

The process seems to be one of problem-solving or hypothesis-testing. The simpler relations are rapidly connected or learned. The more complex, and those where there is a probabilistic relationship, take much longer. A situation where there is error to be accounted for, or where the outcome is only generated some proportion of the times the antecedent conditions occur, requires the collection of many observations. As the hypothesis is being confirmed or denied, as a result of many repetitions, information is flowing and arousal is generated.

To exemplify this, the rhesus monkey studies were cited because the monkeys continued to manipulate the hasps and bolts on a complex box puzzle even when they were not rewarded on completion with a primary reinforcer. White claims this is an example of effectance motivation, the need to produce effects on components of the puzzle.

The arousal-seeking model would explain the problem by pointing out that in the cage it was likely that there were no other more potent sources for arousal-seeking behavior, and that until the monkey reduced the elements of the puzzle box to complete redundancy or familiarity they continued to present some uncertainty and therefore arousal potential.

In fact, the preceding quotation of White continues:

> This [the task of developing an effective *familiarity* with his environment] involves discovering the effects he can have on the environment and the effects the environment will have on him. To the extent that these re-

sults are preserved by learning, they build up an increased competence in dealing with the environment. The child's play can thus be viewed as serious business, though to him it is merely something that is interesting and fun to do [p. 321].

The motive seems clearly stated by White in that it is interesting and fun to do. For the child or monkey that is sufficient. The byproducts may be preserved in learning and lead to competence, but it is going further than necessary to impute effectance as a motive. The "fun" is a positive affect, and "interesting" in this context connotes the maintenance of attention, both of which have been dealt with in the arousal model.

Competence-effectance, and its immediate precursor, the "behavior primacy" concept of Woodworth (1958), seem to have set up a straw man. In a matrix of competing arousing events surrounding a manipulable object, it is simpler to argue that repetitious responding is maintained by weak competition from other elements. Alternatively, it may be that repetition is created by the fact that satisfactory connections between cause and effect have not yet been made and the situation is still being tested.

Boredom and Stereotyped Behavior

When sub-optimally aroused it is assumed that the animal will interact with the environment adaptively to generate an optimally arousing information flow. This assumption depends on the organism having opportunities to generate interactions of sufficient information load to move upward along its arousal function towards the optimal range. In environments of low complexity such as cages, solitary confinement cells, etc., there are severe limitations on the information that can be generated. Dember and Earl (1957) and Sackett (1965) recognized that experience or learning some of the outcomes of interactions within an environment increases the complexity of the organism. Thus, the more things are known, the less information the old interactions with the environment can carry.

In animals constrained within a limited environment affording few opportunities for the development of optimally arousing interactions, another class of nonutilitarian behaviors frequently occurs—stereotyped behavior. Stereotypic behavior has been characterized by Davenport and Menzel as "frequent, almost mechanical, repetition of a posture or movement which varies only slightly in form from time to time, and which serves no obvious functions [1963, p. 99]."

Stereotyped behaviors present a major problem in the management of the animals emitting them since the responses are often repeated so frequently that the animal becomes damaged through wear and tear (Hediger, 1950). Such self-destructive stereotyped behavior is common among institutionalized retarded humans, and the need for improved management procedures is pressing.

Stereotyped behavior is common and has been described in a large variety of zoo animals by Hediger (1950), in chimpanzees (Davenport & Menzel, 1963; Berkson, Mason & Saxon, 1963; Menzel, Davenport & Rogers, 1963; Berkson & Mason, 1964), in canaries (Sargent & Keiper, 1967), chickens (Levy, 1944), in normal children (Olson, 1929; Koch, 1935; Lourie, 1949; Kravitz, Rosenthal & Teplitz, 1960; Gramza, 1970), and in retarded and/or institutionalized children (Levy, 1944; Berkson & Davenport, 1962; Davenport & Berkson, 1963; Hollis, 1965; Hutt & Hutt, 1965; Kaufman & Levitt, 1965; Levitt & Kaufman, 1965). Stereotyped responses may be normal early in development (Gesell & Amatruda, 1941; Lourie, 1949) but they persist in animals reared under aberrant conditions of deprivation (Levy, 1944; Davenport & Menzel, 1963) and in humans exhibiting mental retardation.

The sensoristatic formulation provides an explanation and suggests procedures for their elimination. The limit to the upward trend in organism complexity is reached when the environment ceases to provide pacers, or interactions of appropriate complexity to yield information flow. Under these circumstances stereotypies seem to be the result of chronic states of perceptual deprivation, since it is no longer possible for the organism to generate large enough information loads for optimal arousal. This is supported by the observation that the incidence of stereotypies is inversely related to the opportunities for the animal to indulge in alternate activity (Berkson, Mason & Saxon, 1963; Davenport & Berkson, 1963; Berkson & Mason, 1964).

There is another explanation for the emission of stereotyped behaviors. Berlyne (1960) argues that under conditions of extended reduced stimulation the stimuli that are present are sufficient to prevent sleep, yet not sufficient to maintain the cortical surveillance of the RAS. The RAS is freed from cortical restraint and activates the organism till it enters a state of chronic supra-optimal arousal.

The outcome is that sensory deprivation renders the cortex incapable of counteracting the RAS and is aversive because these internal factors create a level of arousal greater than the optimum. Berlyne argues for this on two grounds. First, the deprived subject does not behave like an animal that is sub-optimally aroused. It shows restlessness, agitation, and eventually disorganization. Second, the electrical activity of the brain indicates a rise in arousal rather than the opposite under these conditions.

This seems to be paradoxical. The lowered level of stimulation eventually becomes so aversive that it becomes arousing in its own right.

At this point, the explanation for stereotyped behaviors is uncertain. We know it occurs under conditions of chronically low information loads, it appears in caged animals, institutionalized retardates, and normal children under boring conditions. It is not known whether it occurs because the subject is chronically supra- or sub-optimally aroused.

Whether it is argued that stereotypy occurs in supra- or sub-optimally aroused animals, prevention appears to lie in the provision of appropriate levels of information for processing. It can be argued that stereotyped behavior is an adaptive response to the situation since even the most stereotyped response carries some information. It is not possible to reproduce a response exactly since the barrage of efferent stimuli must be modified constantly to nullify errors likely to be created by changes in the substrate of conditions from which the response is generated (Bernstein, 1967), i.e., posture, locale, age, fatigue, etc. Thus, perfectly stereotyped responses require the processing of information to allow the nullification of disturbing influences. Information will be generated by the errors contained in each response that must be sensed and corrected to prevent the response drifting off into a different form. Further, the organism can attend selectively to different aspects of the barrage of efferent stimuli resulting from the response. Thus, it seems that expression of stereotyped responses provides the wherewithal for the subject to maintain minimal flow of information under circumstances in which there is limited environmental complexity or perceptual deprivation.

At the moment stereotyped behavior remains enigmatic theoretically, but practically must be viewed as a sign of perceptual deprivation. It can be combated by presentation of opportunities for appropriately arousing alternate activities. The alternate activities offered must clearly reflect the animal's intrinsic capacity to respond to the environment. Thus zoos, prisons, and institutions for retardates must recognize that the alternate activity must present pacer stimuli. The activities must be appropriate and must have the capacity to present appropriate problems for solution, i.e., novelty, complexity, and conflict (as defined here) to maintain an upward trend in the complexity of the animal or person. For example, it is likely that retardates emit stereotyped responses, not because there are not complex stimuli enough in their environments but because they are incapable of systematizing and manipulating the cognitive or symbolic elements that they represent. The behavior of retardates may also be much too simple to provide appropriately arousing stimuli for their attendants and, therefore, social interaction between the child-care workers and the child is minimized. Without the capacity to escalate the complexity of their cognitive interactions in the relatively simple settings of the usual institution, and in the absence of social interactions, the retardate rapidly exhausts the potential of the environment for stimulating interactions at an appropriate level and becomes perceptually deprived.

Stereotyped behaviors, while influenced by some environmental factors, are not immediately contingent on specific stimuli nor do the responses produce contingent changes in the environment. To this end, the behavior satisfies a limited definition of play by being apparently nonutilitarian.

Stereotyped behavior may also be play since it seems, like play, to be related to the problems faced by an organism in maintaining appropriate levels of information flow through its system.

Arousal Avoidance

Play seems to be a word we use to categorize behaviors that elevate arousal. We have no word for the class of behaviors that reduces the level of arousal. Even though arousal avoidance is an important area of concern we have been less interested in it since as humans we can often escape over-arousing situations. Our major struggle is for stimulation (Morris, 1969) but it is necessary to round out the case by including the kinds of behavior that have the opposite effect to play, namely stimulus-avoidance.

The statements made concerning the level of optimal arousal till now have left the word "level" in the singular. However, the precise formulations of the optimal arousal concept use the word "levels," indicating that there is an optimal level for each task (Duffy, 1957; Samuels, 1959; Schultz, 1965; Fiske & Maddi, 1961; Yerkes & Dodson, 1908; Malmo, 1959; Jones, 1969), and that this varies according to concepts like task difficulty. The animal seeks to generate arousal levels appropriate to the task at hand. Thus, supra-optimal arousal is not only aversive but disorganizes or reduces performance. This is expressed as a family of "inverted U" functions relating performance to arousal, each one appropriate for different kinds of tasks (Figure 5.4).

When human operators are bombarded with more information than they are capable of dealing with, the preferred strategy is escape. The subject merely leaves the supra-arousing situation. However, occasionally the subject is prevented from doing this and then performance is disorganized. Analysis of the performance indicates one or more of the following effects as the quantity of information translated from input to response is reduced (Miller, 1960).

 a. omission—failure to transform input into a response, the information is ignored
 b. error—failure to transform the input into the correct response
 c. queueing—the input is held in store till it can be dealt with in turn
 d. filtering—only certain aspects of the input are attended to

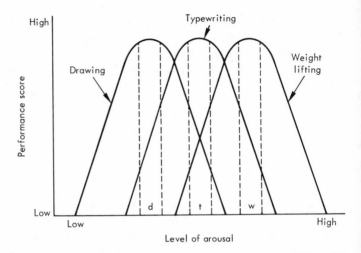

Figure 5.4
Relation between level of arousal and performance. Curves
showing hypothetical relations between level of arousal
and performance. Ranges (D, T, W) of optimal levels of
arousal for performance on three different tasks. From
D. Bindra, *Motivation—A Systematic Reinterpretation.* New
York: Ronald Press Company. Copyright, 1959.

   e. reduction of discrimination—the input is not treated at a fine enough
level of discrimination, e.g., instead of reacting "I see yellow," the
subject says, "I see color"

   f. decentralization—the input is deployed into multiple channels

Chronic inescapable supra-optimal arousal with its attendant chain of
autonomic alterations of the physiology lead to the stress diseases that are
common in the adults of some societies where the information load (novelty, uncertainty, complexity) on individuals is high.

   Much less attention has been given to this area of concern, although
there is some data that deals with the effect of personality on the strategies people use to modify the uncertainties of their behavior. The risk-
taking models of behavior advanced by Atkinson (1957) predict which
types of people prefer high levels of uncertainty or information flow and
vice versa, but there does not seem to be a consistent thread running
through a body of research that deals with anti-play, the behaviors concerned with the reduction of arousal.

Redefinition of Play

   Stimulus-seeking and play have much in common: they occur when
they are not preempted by the need to satisfy prepotent drives; they are

accompanied by positive affect; they both involve exploration, investigation, and manipulation of the environment or the symbolic representations of experience; and such stimulus-seeking and play behaviors that are observable are both emitted with higher frequency by the young of a species. The similarities between them lead to the obvious question, "Are they not the same phenomenon?" The answer seems to be that play is clearly stimulus-seeking behavior, yet not all stimulus-seeking behavior is play if we insist that play is not related directly to the survival of the player (see Table 5.1, p. 111 for a summary of the assumptions and criticisms of the two modern theories).

Assuming that there is a sensoristatic drive, much of the activity of the animal may satisfy a primary drive while providing interactions with the environment that promote optimal arousal. Since this behavior is linked to survival and is serious, most observers would classify it as work. Only that behavior that seems to be clearly nonutilitarian is play (or not work). This definition of play is dependent on the behavior's uselessness to the animal as imputed by the observer. Long ago Schlosberg (1947) drew our attention to the circularity of saying that play is play because the observer thinks it is.

Play is an artificial category. It is merely that part of stimulus-seeking behavior to which we cannot ascribe a prepotent motive. In trying to set it apart as a watertight category our understanding is clouded with the efforts necessary to seek the discriminants that differentiate work from play. We are led into an artificial dichotomization of the behavior into work and play, when clearly some behavior can be both. Any juxtaposition of work and play must be along a continuum with serious or critical behavior at one pole and behavior that serves only to maintain arousal and no other effect at the other.

It is more simple to adopt a view of animals as driven to interact with their environments by their needs to maintain their separate integrity as organisms. Activity is intimately tied to the processes of growth and maintenance. One of the drives serving these processes is the need to process information to maintain optimal arousal levels. The animal will indulge in interactions that lead to the elevation of arousal level when possible.

In the normal environment of a neophilic animal the opportunities for stimulus-seeking are good and the exigencies of change encourage its practice. However, stimulus-seeking may not occur for a variety of reasons. Stimulus-seeking activity may be preempted by stronger incentives to emit responses that are tied to other needs, or the contingencies may be such that it is punished. Alternatively, there may be no opportunities to indulge in stimulus-seeking because the environment is so simple and well-known that there may be no interactions available which carry information or arousal potential.

A definition for play then becomes: *play is that behavior that is motivated by the need to elevate the level of arousal towards the optimal.* This definition shares the problem of previous definitions in that it depends on the imputation of the motive by the observer. However, it goes a long way further in specifying the conditions under which play is likely to occur. Its corollary, *work is the behavior emitted to reduce the level of stimulation,* fits nicely the concept of drive-reduction theories of behavior.

Since both activities are necessary to the health of the organism, both could be considered work. This clearly identifies where the problem lies in defining work and play. The problem lies in the imputation by the observer that certain behaviors look as though they are tied directly to life support, and are therefore important or work. The other behaviors, interpreted as playful because they are apparently not directly related to life support, are seen as play. When playful behaviors are accorded the status of necessary activities, then play becomes work and the meaning in this play/work dichotomy drops out.

If play is stimulus-seeking behavior and if work is life-supporting behavior, many, many activities are both at the same time. Frequently, the life-support activities are sufficiently interesting to allow the worker to maintain his arousal level while earning the monetary rewards necessary for existence.

There exists a choice in defining play. We can insist on forcing it to become a conceptual opposite of work, or we can face the complexity of the problem. A behavior may have many motives that are not mutually exclusive and an adequate explanation must recognize this. One of the drives maintaining behavior is the need to optimize arousal, which does not exclude the possibility that the same behavior may anticipate and account for a potential need. The contributions of the various drives to a behavior will be difficult to disentangle.

It seems that pure play can occur only when all extrinsic consequences are eliminated and the behavior is driven on solely by intrinsic motivation. Pure play is probably only theoretically possible and striving for a pure definition only makes sense in that context.

More important than the struggle for a watertight definition is the struggle for an understanding of the relationships between the antecedent conditions, the hypothetical drives and the resulting behavior that satisfies them. The work on the information drive that has been gaining momentum since World War II provides many of these links at both the theoretical and empirical levels. Play and work lie on a continuum.

Table 5.1

Modern Theories

NAME	PLAY IS CAUSED:	THIS EXPLANATION ASSUMES THAT:	IT CAN BE CRITICIZED BECAUSE:
12. Play as Arousal-Seeking	by the need to generate interactions with the environment or self that elevate arousal (level of interest or stimulation) towards the optimal for the individual	1. there is a need for optimal arousal 2. change in arousal towards optimal is pleasant 3. the organism learns the behaviors that result in that feeling and vice versa 4. stimuli vary in their capacity to arouse 5. stimuli that arouse are those involving novelty, complexity, and/or dissonance, i.e., information 6. the organism will be forced to emit changing behavior and maintain engagement with arousing stimuli	1. it is very general but it handles questions of work and play equally well. In fact it questions the validity of separating work from play
13. Competence/Effectance	by a need to produce effects in the environment. Such effects demonstrate competence and result in feelings of effectance	1. demonstration of competence leads to feelings of effectance 2. effectance is pleasant 3. effectance increases the probability of tests of competence	1. for the organism to constantly test whether it can still competently produce an effect seems to require uncertainty as to the outcome. Uncertainty or information seem to be the very attributes of stimuli that are arousing 2. it can be argued that competence/effectance behavior is a kind of arousal-seeking

AN INTEGRATION

Chapter 6

Ragheb (1971), in a term paper attempting to integrate the many theories of play, started by considering the question of why the various theories had not yet been satisfactorily integrated into at least fewer but more inclusive formulations. He gave several reasons:

First, play is a complex phenomenon with many variables and manifestations. Consideration of a few of these factors leads to a limited explanation. The surplus-energy theory is a prime example of an explanation for some behavior made from an extremely limited view of play behavior that considered essentially one factor—the patterns of energy expenditure.

Secondly, theorists have, in general, approached their explanations with a view blinkered by their academic affiliation with a discipline. Thus there are physiological, psychological, sociological explanations.

Thirdly, since the organisms observed grow along some trajectory of development it is possible to force on to that trajectory separate stages of development. When this has been done, several theorists have been content to try to explain playful behavior within the limits of one or more of the stages. For example, the compensation and generalization theories do not seem to apply to preschoolers.

Fourthly, the early theories of play tended to be merely ingredients in a broad theoretical conception of behavior. The question of play was not central to any of the theories. Thus most formulations concerning play have come as spinoffs from efforts to explain other elements in behavior. The older theorists did not deal with play explicitly as a complex and attempted an integrated explanation. As a result of the early theorists, modern views have tried to specify more directly the phenomena of concern in such a way that testable hypotheses might be generated. Their work has led away from the old grand schemata and generated more data but has yet to produce an integrated explanation of the motive and role of play.

Lastly, methodological difficulties, and difficulties in persuading peers and funding agencies that play is a class of behaviors worthy of serious attention, have militated against a concerted theoretical and empirical push into the realms of play behavior.

For all of these reasons there have been few earnest attempts to deal with the problem of integrating some of the limited explanations already dealt with into a more inclusive and comprehensive statement concerning the motive for and the content of play behavior.

The preceding chapters have dealt with the many explanations of the motive for and content of play. There can be two reactions: One is that all but one explanation must be wrong and the other, that the best explanation lies in some composite or integration of several of these explanations. This chapter adopts the latter view and attempts to build an integrated explanation from some of the preceding explanations.

Play and Evolution

To start at the beginning, it is clear that players inherit many factors which influence their behavior. Each individual is the product of germ plasm determined by aeons of selective pressure towards adaptation to an environmental niche. The genotype is a powerful influence upon which are superimposed the accumulated effects of the unique experiences of the individual since conception. We have, of late, tended to down-play the genotype as a contributor, presumably because we can do little about it, and have heaped our attention on the phenotype since we can presumably affect it by means of our influence over an individual's experiences. We have tended to forget that an individual and his behavior result from an interaction between these two classes of influence on behavior. Lockard (1971) and Kohlberg (1968) argue the point more extensively, but this integration starts from that point of interaction.

The inherited influences can be considered as those that unite a species and those that separate its members. For example, man has attributes that set him apart from other species. His bipedalism, his highly developed forebrain, relative hairlessness, and a myriad of other elements, make man man and not chimpanzee. Yet among men there is great variability at least in part directly ascribable to the genetic inheritance of each individual.

Man lives where it is advantageous to be flexible in behavior. Man can tolerate large and rapid change in his circumstances today because similar changes in the past have selected against those who could not tolerate the changeability. So we come to the present, each of us the fruits of selection, all to some extent ready for an existence encompassing change and requiring behavioral flexibility. Thus to varying degrees we are neophilic.

The Inheritance of Capacity to Change

The question arises, "How do we inherit the effector organs and responses necessary for the new conditions ahead that by definition can not yet be defined?" This question was first faced but not answered satisfactorily in the theory of play as preparation. The solution is relatively simple. All that is needed is to breed into the germ plasm a predisposition to be rewarded by the emission of new responses and the occurrence of novel stimulus events.

This reinforcement of behavior leading to novel sensations will naturally increase the probability of novel responses by virtue of the Law of Effect. Individuals that have generated relatively large numbers of novel responses over and above those required for immediate existence will acquire information as a byproduct that will tend to convey an advantage when circumstances change. In other words, the more neophilic the species and individual the greater chance it will have of surviving change in its habitat.

However, even new responses will be subject to the array of consequences generated by the existing circumstances. Thus if the new response ignores gravity, the need for oxygen and nutrients, warmth, shelter, etc., the resulting deleterious effects will be sensed by the systems of primary reinforcement. If the reward from achieving a new response is outweighed by its aversive consequences, it will be extinguished. Thus the joint action of the consequences of the current circumstances and the tendency to emit novel responses will tune the behavior of the individual to its particular circumstances. It will keep the individual in a state of behavioral flux so that it may keep pace with change in its niche.

Ashby in his book *Design for a Brain* (1960) raised exactly this issue. How can the germ plasm, which is dependent for its creation on the existence of like conditions for generations, deal with the specificities of each unique circumstance? Ashby defined two kinds of events or disturbances against which the animal had to defend itself. The first set were constant and required a constant defense. He used the example of a foreign body in the trachea and the reflex response of the cough. It was enough in general for the animal to cough and those that could cough survived. He called this a direct defense.

The earlier forms of gene-pattern adapted in this way only. The later forms, however, have developed a specialization that can give them a defense against a class of disturbances to which the earlier were vulnerable. This class consists of those disturbances that, although not constant over a span of many generations (and thus not adaptable to by the gene-pattern, for the change is too rapid) are none the less constant over a span of a single generation. When disturbances of this class are frequent, there is advantage in the development of an adapting mechanism that is (1) controlled in its outlines by the gene-pattern (for the same outlines are wanted over many generations), and (2) controlled in details by the details applicable to that particular generation.

This is the learning mechanism. Its peculiarity is that the gene-pattern delegates part of its control over the organism to the environment. Thus, it does not specify in detail how a kitten shall catch a mouse, but provides a learning mechanism and a tendency to play, so that it is *the mouse* which teaches the kitten the finer points of how to catch mice. This is regulation, or adaptation, by the indirect method. The gene-pattern does not, as it were, dictate, but puts the kitten into the way of being able to form its own adaptation, guided in detail by the environment [Ashby, 1960, p. 234].

Ashby's question can be extended. It could be asked, "What inheritable mechanism would enable a species to adapt directly to conditions that require it be flexible?" If this question could be answered then we might be able to explain more than the specificities of a particular kitten's responses to a set of mice. Just such an inheritable mechanism was described in Chapter 5, in the analysis of play as arousal-seeking. This model for the mechanisms during the behavior of the higher animals seems to achieve exactly what is needed. They seem to be the mechanisms necessary to push the animal continuously into engagements with the environment. The engagements are rewarding if they tend to move the animal towards optimal arousal, and since the arousal potential of such an interaction depends on its novelty, complexity, or dissonance, then the animal is in constant contact with the elements in its environment that are changing or are changeable. In the evolution of playing animals there seem to have developed mechanisms that lead to play or arousal-seeking behavior under circumstances where the prepotent physiological drives ensuring immediate survival of the individual were suspended. Play behavior has adaptive significance for the individual by broadening the breadth of experience the individual has to draw on in meeting the challenge of change. The animals that survive to breed tend to pass on their inherited predispositions to play, thus influencing the playfulness of the species.

Thus, stimulus events and configurations in the environment that are novel, complex, and dissonant elevate arousal and to the extent this moves an individual towards an optimal level it is accompanied by positive affect or pleasure. The kinds of behaviors engendered by such reinforcement are exploration, investigation, and manipulation. This process leads to increased knowledge of the conditions and consequences of the environment over and above the immediate satisfaction of basic survival needs. Play fosters the behavioral variability of an individual, and therefore a species, and thereby increases the probability of future adaptation to unpredictable circumstances. Play is behavior that, in Ashby's terms, results in indirect adaptation to circumstances where behavioral flexibility is an advantage.

Variability in Play

Breeding patterns and the principles of reproductive physiology ensure among-individual variability for all characteristics of a species. Thus great variability can be expected in form and behavior among the individuals of a species. Individual differences in tolerance for sub-optimal arousal and the optimal level for arousal are to be expected in just the same way that needs for oxygen, warmth, etc., vary. The joint action of all of these motivating factors makes each individual a unique clustering of behavioral tendencies. Therefore playfulness can be expected to vary along all its dimensions like other characteristics.

The inherited predispositions described above are enough to provide for the individual variability necessary for the survival of the species. However, once individuals are conceived their behavior is shaped by the accumulations of their experience. The variable behaviors emitted are met by a variety of consequences that continuously mold that behavior in given directions.

Learning and Play

At the simplest level these consequences stem from the physical world and the current limitations of the individual's own morphology and physiology via the primary needs and their reinforcers. At a higher level, among social animals at least, there also operate the secondary social reinforcers that condition behavior. Thus, from the beginning, the behavior engendered in the mother by her child's responses tends in turn to reinforce certain of the child's responses. As a human youngster grows the constellation of reinforcing and extinguishing elements in the everyday life of a family of a given class, race, and religion, located in a particular region within a nation, all demand behavioral adaptations by the individuals.

The interaction of inherited tendencies of individuals and the exigencies of their particular situations generate individuals fitted to their current situations to varying extents. Differing capacities to learn, differing tendencies to engage in new interactions with the environment, and differing applications of social consequences by others sharing a· niche, will all contribute to a variation in adaptation.

Thus, the arousal-seeking model provides a motivational system that reinforces behavioral flexibility. From the large variety of possible behaviors the complex of primary and secondary positive and negative reinforcers selects those appropriate for the survival of an individual. However, the continued need for arousing stimuli will maintain the tendency for behavioral change.

Development—Inheritance and Experience

The last factor to be integrated concerns the increase in complexity of individuals as they accumulate experiences. Experiences are probably best defined as remembered relationships between responses and consequences. Thus with an increasing number of experiences individuals can make more reliable predictions as to probable outcomes of responses. They can deal with more complex assemblages or chains of such relationships. They accumulate more experiential data on which to base their behavior and the complexity of their behavior increases accordingly. This concept of upwardly spiraling complexity is explained by the "pacer" concept of Dember and Earl (1957) and Sackett (1965) referred to earlier.

To summarize, individual members of some species inherit predispositions to emit new responses because they are pleasurable. The interaction of this tendency with the consequences of behavior in a particular setting, tune the individual's behavior to that setting while retaining the capacity for adaptation to change. At birth the young individual begins the process of acquiring and remembering (learning) the relationships between myriads of responses and outcomes, gradually acquiring the capacity to make more reliable predictions and to chain together strings of symbolic abstractions. As a result, with experience the individual becomes more intimately adapted to its setting. To the extent that a particular niche requires the individuals of a species to develop along a developmental trajectory in common with other individuals, then it is possible to classify the course of the development into developmental stages.

This developmental view is not at heart theoretical; it is descriptive. It points to a common pathway, and predicts what is likely to happen to a child on the basis of what has happened to children before. It is extremely valuable however. The genotype of the next generation will be similar to the last, and the factors in a particular society will also be somewhat similar. It is possible, therefore, to make predictions based on the assumption that the new children will be similar to the current group.

The formulations of play as caused by arousal-seeking and learning and the cognitive dynamics of development can be integrated in this way. The arousal-seeking model explains the mechanism driving the individual into engagement with the environment in ways surplus to the need of immediate survival. The consequences of such behavior comes, via learning, to condition the content of the behavior so motivated. The accumulative effect of such learning interacts with the arousal-seeking motive to produce an upward spiral in the complexity of the interactions. Similarities in that developmental path have led to the separation of the continuous process of growth into developmental stages where growing individuals are seen to move through similar phases at approximately the same time.

IMPLICATIONS
FOR PRACTICE

Chapter 7

The preceding chapters have established clearly that most of the explanations for play are unacceptable. The most satisfying explanation seems to involve an integration of three: play as arousal-seeking, play as learning, and the developmentalist view of the child. This integration uses interrelationships between the motive for play, the constraints placed on expression of playful responses by the environment, and the effects they work on the complexity of children to explain play behavior. It is the purpose of this chapter to take that integrated explanation, or theory, and apply it to some of the situations in which people play. Such applications are necessary so that those influencing the play of humans can preserve the basic characteristics of play and therefore its desirable outcomes.

This smacks of recipes, and recipes are dangerous. Earlier it was stated that the output from a theoretician should become the input of the practitioner. In other words, the practitioners, the only ones who appreciate the specificities of their situations, must make the final jump from an understanding of a principle to its application. Recipes preempt that process. Recipes are general prescriptions and must ignore the unique elements existing at their point of application. Recipes and prescriptions will be avoided, but clearly the formulations advanced in Chapters 5 and 6 can be applied to the variety of settings in which children play in order to derive some general principles for the operation of those settings.

Much of this chapter is speculative. It has been written using an imagination fettered by the insights provided by the evaluation of the various explanations for play, and insights concerning the nature and goals of the various settings for play. It is, in fact, a personal statement.

People at Work or Play

Educational and recreational institutions are not far apart in their contents and methods. Both sets of institutions produce relatively permanent changes in individuals' behavior, or learning. Schools avowedly set out to do so and often use play as a way to produce learning. Recreation sets out in search of play, and often reaches it by providing situations in which learning takes place. The communality in content and method stems from the nature of the people they serve. The clients do not change in nature because they are in school or at play. The people, children and adults, remain the same complex organisms whether at work or play.

Education is concerned with preparation and recreation with living here and now. In the school play is justified from the viewpoint that its byproducts will be useful later. In recreation play is justified because it is accompanied by immediate benefits. In both cases, the managers of the setting, teachers or recreation leaders, must wrestle with the problems of managing the situation to realize their goals. The determination of those goals is the major problem. The following section deals extensively with the problem of determining whether the person is or should be playing or working. It is written with teachers, recreation workers, and mothers in mind because these leaders are charged with the management of environments in which others work and play. It is necessary for them to recognize the differences between behavior that is extrinsically and intrinsically motivated.

Since school programs and recreation programs are discriminable in their intent, if not necessarily by their content, the following discussion separates them for convenience. The discussion is applied directly to a school setting, but its principles are picked up again later in the chapter when they are incorporated into a discussion of leisure behavior. Further, although the discussion deals with children, the same principles apply to adults and again will be referred to later.

Teachers have to wrestle with the problem of deciding whether to teach specific responses or to develop in individuals a capacity to deal afresh with the problems that beset them. The problem can be simplified to the extent that they can identify with some certainty the responses that will be critical for the survival of the society and the individual within it. However, the problem of how to prepare the individual for conditions in which many of the circumstances are as yet undefined is just as critical. It is as part of the process of preparation for the unknown that play seems to be important.

The use of play in education and recreation is dependent on the recognition that the playful attitude is a worthy and productive one. Lieberman (1965, 1966), cited earlier, equated playfulness and creativity. The playful attitude, an indifference to extrinsic payoffs, allows a new response for the person or a new (for that person) transformation of information. Novel engagements with elements in the environment are self-reinforcing and sustain the behavior leading to new knowledge. People do not need extrinsic rewards to engage with and learn about the environment.

This need to play provides a method for the leader to respect individuality of people while dealing with them in groups. Even if our educational institutions were not concerned with fostering individuality and attempted the most rigorously controlled situation each person would still represent a unique blend of genetic and experiential effects. This suggests that stereotyped procedures for dealing with people simultaneously and similarly are fraught with problems stemming from their variance. Since play is a process that is sustained by intrinsic motives and utilizes content determined by individuals, it is unique to them. At one stroke play fosters individuality and provides children with learnings that reflect their unique requirements, not some uneasy average.

If the specific responses necessary for the survival of a person in the culture can be defined, then the laws of learning can be applied to ensure that the individual acquires them as expeditiously as possible. Here clearly the person can be made to work towards appropriate responses by the establishment of consequences or contingencies. For example, it is clear that our children must learn to speak and read at least English if their life opportunities are not to be constrained later. They must also learn some arithmetic, the monetary system, traffic regulations, and so on. If a specific behavior can be determined, according to the exigencies of immediate circumstances and local philosophies, then the task of teaching them to the child is relatively easy. At the same time there must exist a concern for preparing the child for the unknown. This is as important but is more difficult and can only be achieved by different tactics.

Between the poles of certainty concerning what is desired of a person and the uncertainty concerning what responses will be adaptive in the years hence, lies a middle-ground fraught with tension. In the middle lie the responses that might have use later. They raise the question whether the child should be taught them formally, or merely be taught the processes whereby such problems or responses can be acquired should they become relevant. Obviously the question is unanswerable in a general sense, but it is resolvable in a specific location in terms of the local philosophies concerning what is desirable.

These issues can be crystallized by arranging the functions of an educational institution on a continuum from training through problem-

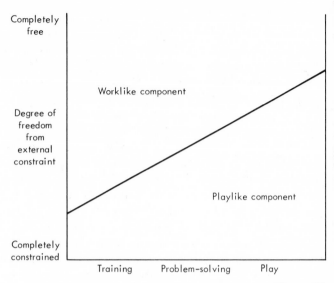

Figure 7.1
The Educational Continuum (From Banks, 1972).

solving to play (Banks, 1972), as shown in Figure 7.1. In the first case, the task is clear; to induce specific responses by training. In the middle zone, the responses have some probability of being desirable, and are used as the outcomes to be sought for in a problem-solving approach. Here latitude in the manner of achievement is allowed, but constraints on the possible solutions exist. Towards the other pole the goals of the behavior and the manner in which they are sought are freed as far as possible from constraint. It is at this end that playful or creative behavior is to be encouraged.

Given that some responses such as reading are sufficiently complex to require the long accumulation of experiences over hundreds of days, each day should balance the requirement for work towards a specific goal and play towards the undefinable goals.

At any given time it should be possible for the educator to decide whether the child should be at work on the acquisition of a defined response, practicing problem-solving, or playing. That decision is a difficult but crucial one since it materially changes the definitions of an acceptable response. What might be an error subject to negative consequences in a training situation could be an acceptable and creative response during play.

Passing the responsibility for the decision of which responses are to be required to a local practitioner is necessary in a pluralistic society. However, it is possible to decree that each educational or socializing institution or individual must balance preparation for the known with that for the unknown; it must balance work and play. Thus in each setting there must be provision for and encouragement of playful activity. Achieving that is the problem.

The various circumstances in which it is hoped that play will take place may not in fact allow the expression of that behavior. Play will not occur when the essential conditions necessary for play behavior are absent. First, unsatisfied primary and acquired drives can preempt playful behavior. The point was brought home strongly in the 1970 White House Conference on Children (Anon, 1970) that before the children can be freed to play their basic needs for food, health, warmth, security, etc., must have been met. The delegates were concerned with recognizing that the lack of basic ingredients for healthy living would preempt the emission of play and thereby work a double injury to disadvantaged children.

Secondly, given the satisfaction of these requirements, there are other conditions necessary for the emission of playful behavior. These additional conditions have been identified by Neumann (1971) in a way that is consistent with the historical definitions of play. Neumann analyzed at great length the writings on play and derived a set of criteria that when satisfied would set play apart from non-play. The criteria are valuable in that they allow a practitioner to quickly, albeit subjectively, evaluate whether the behavior is playful or not, and suggest from first principles how to modify the setting so that play is permitted.

The criteria are locus of control of the player, the nature of the motive for the behavior, and the necessary constraints of reality. Briefly put, if the locus of control of the behavior is vested in the individual, if the behavior is intrinsically motivated, then the behavior is play. These criteria are closely related and deal with the motive for the behavior. Children are playing when control of the content of their behavior is largely under their control. The child is playing when the motive for the behavior is intrinsic to the process of the behavior itself and there are no critical deferred or immediate rewards imposed from outside. Neumann added a further criterion. The child should transcend the immediate constraints of the reality of the situation when playing. Imaginary or cognitive extensions of previous experiences should appear. Daydreams or fantasies or epistemic behavior are important ingredients comprising a final stage of a play episode.

Neumann set up these criteria as guides to the practitioner. It cannot be conclusively determined whether the criteria are satisfied, but these three principles provide appropriate questions for a leader or teacher to ask about a situation in which play behavior is appropriate or desired. The questions do not require lengthy analysis of a situation, but rest upon the judgments and insights of an observer who cannot afford the luxury of extended observation. The pace of events is too fast for a practitioner to do more than practice, as skillfully as possible, the art of making snap corrections in a situation as events develop. The criteria help the practitioner improve the probability of making a series of correct judgments. Now to deal with these criteria in more detail.

In general, play has been characterized as behavior in which the player is freed as far as possible from constraints imposed upon which response is to be made to a given set of antecedent events. Obviously all constraints cannot be removed, so the question really becomes to what extent can the setting permit playful behavior. When play is desired, then the conditions need to be set so that as many constraints as possible are removed. This is the point behind Neumann's criteria. They suggest ways of maximizing the playfulness of a setting.

If the behavior is motivated intrinsically then given the other conditions, the child may behave playfully. Intrinsic motivation has been discussed at length. The arousal-seeking model attempts to explain the mystery of behavior that is apparently unmotivated. The player is emitting the behavior for the rewards associated with the processes of its emission rather than with the end product. To this, Neumann adds the question, "Does the locus of control lie within the player?" The degree to which control is passed to an outside agent determines the degree to which the behavior is not playful. Again this suggests a continuum from maximal internal control where responses are limited only by the physical properties of the environment, through cooperative play where some control is passed to others in the play setting, to a situation where the player is merely executing the requirements of an outside agent, such as a teacher or mother.

Neumann's final question concerned the degree to which the play is tied to an external reality. If the player could suspend some of the external realities of the situation and was allowed to behave to some extent independently of those constraints, then the behavior would be playful. Make-believe suspension of some of the constraints of reality makes for play.

These three criteria are attempts to establish principles for actively freeing the play settings of external constraints. They are all very closely related and assume that what has to be done to allow play to occur is to free the player from constraint and rely on the strong arousal-seeking drive to propel the child into playful interactions. They follow closely from the general form of the definition of play; play is the behavior that is intrinsically motivated.

The questions relevant to a practical setting that derive directly from the criteria are simple and they can be applied to determine whether the child is playing, or to determine the conditions in which it is hoped a child will play. Taking Neumann's criteria and applying them to the question whether the child is playing, the following pairs of questions are examples:

1a. Is the child undertaking the behavior in order to achieve a payoff? or
1b. Is the child behaving only for the experiential rewards associated with the process?

Both of these questions can be unified and extended by asking whether the behavior would continue if the payoff or final contingency were re-. moved. If the child can be expected to continue to emit the behavior, then it can be inferred that the process is sufficiently rewarding in itself; that it is intrinsically motivated.

2a. Is the behavior controlled by somebody other than the child? or
2b. Is the child himself controlling the behavior?

Both of these questions attack who is determining the nature, extent, and direction of the behavior. If it seems to be the child himself, or at least if no other person seems to be directing the behavior, then control is probably located in the individual.

3a. Is the child forced by circumstance to recognize all the constraints of reality? or
3b. Is it possible for the child to bend some aspects of the real situation by suspending temporarily associations between events in favor of an imagined situation?

These questions refer obviously to fantasy or imagination and can be derived from Piaget's concept of play as a predominance of assimilation rather than accommodation.

Turning the questioning to the setting rather than the child, the following pairs of questions may be asked:

4a. Does the setting or situation, including adults, impose consequences that by requiring given behaviors prevent children's concern for the process of their behavior?
4b. Does the setting provide interactions that are freed from an externally applied final consequence?

These questions derive from a concern to allow intrinsically motivated behaviors to occur. It is difficult to avoid attaching consequences to certain behaviors, but doing so endangers play behavior. Separating circumstances where the setting is being manipulated to produce a given behavior from those where unique or creative behavior is desirable is the first step. In the former, learning a definite response is aided by attaching consequences to correct and incorrect responses. In play, the definition of right or wrong lies with the individual.

    5a. Is something in the setting so constraining the behavior that the choices among responses available to the individual are limited?

    5b. Does the setting permit the choices at each choice point in a stream of behavior to rest with the individual?

Obviously these questions concern the location of control, and with passing it to the child.

    6a. Does the setting prevent a relaxation from a concern with the real connections between events and consequences? or

    6b. Does it allow the suspension of some aspects of reality?

All of these questions are general and are rather redundant but they bear on the extent to which the child can be characterized as working or playing in the sense that his behavior is externally or internally determined. At this point it must be reemphasized that no setting can be so arranged that a child can be totally freed from external constraints. What is expected to result from the questions is the removal of unnecessary constraints so that there is an improved probability that the child will emit the kinds of responses that seem to be driven by the need to play. The arousal-seeking motive demands the reduction of uncertainty or the processing of information. It elicits novel and increasingly complex and dissonant explorations, investigations, manipulations of the setting. What is novel, complex, or dissonant is determined by the unique phenotype of the individual, not by an outside agent.

    The curriculum and organization of a classroom should reflect a conscious identification of the work-like elements in the day's activities by teachers. They should determine beforehand when they are seeking specific responses that they are confident will convey an advantage in the future. These necessary behaviors or knowledges should be identified for the children. The problem then facing the child is clear and becomes "How shall I behave in order to produce a specified response?" Variations in procedures lead to different outcomes which are classified as error. Under these circumstances the set towards the feedback from the teacher during this process tends to move the children towards conformity in their behavior. The ultimate result is that all children solve the same problem using the same prescribed strategy. This kind of behavior is end-oriented, dominated by extrinsic consequences attached to a specific solution.

However, education must promote creativity or the capacity to generate new responses. Only under these circumstances can we survive. Many of the activities in a classroom should not have consequences tied to specific ends. What is needed are reinforcements attached to the attributes of responses rather than the responses themselves. Thus in a setting or activity where children are dealing with problems that are relevant to their own experiences and capacities, praise should be attached to the way in which the problem was solved and the characteristics of the solution. Creativity, novelty, elegance, or simplicity of both process and outcome in terms of the individual child should be the prime concern. Since a creative solution accounts for the necessary constraints in a solution without imposing unnecessary ones, the teacher in disbursing reinforcement must be careful to define the constraints on the possible solutions in terms of the children. What was elegant or novel or creative for them must be rewarded. To add adult or culturally oriented constraints to solutions is to circumscribe the possible responses and over time place limits on the potential creativity of the child.

Thus the playful response is essentially a creative one in which new elements are interwoven with past experiences. A creative response exercises an individual's behavioral flexibility; a highly desirable characteristic for humans. It is all too easy to preempt a creative response or to fail to appreciate one when it occurs. Asking these questions about a home setting, a school room, or a recreation program should help a practitioner to identify those segments of children's lives where they are free to play, and to modify setting to allow playful responses when they are desired.

Play in the Home

The critical effect of early experiences on the later development of the child has been documented well nigh exhaustively by now. Bloom (1964) estimated that by the age of four, half the child's intelligence had been developed, and that the plasticity, or adaptability, wanes with advancing age. This estimation has been backed by many studies and observations showing the marked effects of early environmental deprivation.

For example, some studies point to the need for quite specific experiences. Chimps denied vision or sensation in their forelimbs when very young never quite compensated from their impoverished experiences later. Dogs reared alone under conditions of severe sensory restriction were not able to learn satisfactorily the connection between a noxious stimulus, say fire, and a result, the burnt nose, and to avoid the source of damage. These studies involve the heroic measures of functionally sacrificing the animal to complete a controlled elimination of certain stimuli from the experience of the animal.

On the opposite tack, for example, rats that have experienced a rather general environmental enrichment of their living quarters have consistently shown significant histological and biochemical differences from similar rats deprived of the experiences (Bennett & Rosenzweig, 1968). The enrichment used by the experimenters involved essentially the building of a complex rat-scaled playground in a communal living cage.

Post hoc observations on the state of humans deprived of appropriate early experiences started with the early work of Dennis (1941) who noted that infants in a crowded orphanage in Teheran were not developing physically and socially, despite the fact that their health was satisfactory. The retardation in their development was shown to be created by the almost complete sensory deprivation of each child. They lay in cribs undisturbed except for feeding and toileting. Other reports of similar naturally occurring deprivations of experience and their resulting effects on human and animal development are in the literature.

These studies are far too numerous to describe here and others have already reviewed them (Glass, 1968; Mason, 1971; Weikart & Lambie, 1970; Painter, 1968; Gray & Miller, 1967; Bronfenbrenner, 1968; Gewirtz, 1968; Thompson & Schaefer, 1961). The consensus of these enrichment/ deprivation studies points clearly to the need for experiences or sensory input from engagements with the environment if the animal or human is to develop appropriately.

The moral of the story is clear. Humans, just like the sacrificial laboratory animals in experiments, are susceptible to early deprivation, and if it has proved severe enough, do not recover. The exact timing, duration, and nature of the experiences have not yet been clearly identified, even for rats (Krech, 1969), and we are at a stage in time where it seems wise to engage in generalized enrichment. Krech called this the "kitchen sink" approach to environmental enrichment—a little of everything is thrown in to make sure.

The importance of the early experiences for the development of the very young child is clear. From sense data resulting from his experiences the very young child constructs the basic cognitive or symbolic connections between events that provide the foundations for later development. The influences on the very young child stem largely from the mother in our society, and there are growing attempts to provide the mothering-one with guidance as to provision of a "kitchen sink" full of early experiences. It boils down to a concern for what the mother or parent actually does with the child and not for their socioeconomic status and so on. Wolf (1964) clearly identified the difference between what he called process variables and status variables in the development of the child. Social class, race, and region are all status variables from which, by a process of stereotyping, we are expected to infer things about the behavior of the people so labelled. A more sensible, but of course more difficult procedure, is to look at the actual behavior of the individuals influencing each other. From this it can be determined in what ways the people condition the behavior of others.

Wolf was concerned with intellectual development and identified what he called the "process variables" of press for language, press for achievement motivation and also for general learning. Presumably there are many other unidentified "pressures" that could be identified as process variables influencing the development of the child. These pressures result from attitudes of parents about what is important and therefore condition in turn their behavior towards the child. This section is clearly an attempt to change attitudes of parents towards play. The reason is simple. Play produces adaptations in the behavior of the child and these adaptations result from and contribute to the developing cognitive structure of the child. Exemplifying this concern, other books have recently appeared offering what is in effect a curriculum of playlike activities (Gordon, 1970; Painter, 1971) to stimulate playful engagement between the parent, the child, and elements in their world. In Wolf's language there is a developing conception of a process variable that perhaps could be called a "press for play." Parents, or more sensibly the "mothering-ones," should actively seek to create situations where the child is given opportunities to explore, investigate, and manipulate the items in their world. Further, the items furnished the child should present "pacer" stimuli. The items should allow the child to experience novelty, and/or increasing complexity and dissonance. In other words, they should possess arousal potential or impact by requiring the processing of information.

Thus even in the early life of the child it should be possible to identify whether the child is free to play or is engaged in activity directed by some external agent. Life-support activities, the press to acquire language and other skills, including perhaps a curriculum of playlike activities like Gordon's, should be classified as work. The Neumann criteria would show them to be extrinsically motivated.

The "press for play" has not been identified formally in the analysis of rearing style and its effects on the development of the child. However, a recent study by Bishop and Chace (1971) came close by exemplifying the relationships between parental attitudes to world events, to play and their provisions for play and the playfulness and the effects on the creativity of their child. Bishop and Chace were interested in following a chain of circumstances to see if they would surface in the play behavior of children. The chain was conceived as follows:

1. Parents would vary in the style or manner in which they thought about the world around them and they could be placed on a continuum. At one end the parents would be concrete thinkers, using rules, principles, dogma, and precedent to govern their lives and thinking. Towards the abstract end parents would tend to be more flexible, thinking things out afresh when faced with new situations.
2. The play environment these parents would provide would reflect their conceptual systems.
3. The rearing environment established by parents would influence the conceptual systems and hence behavior of the child.

To trace this chain the authors investigated the attitudes of the parents on a questionnaire to a variety of currently interesting but controversial issues. The answers revealed the parents' attitudes and systems of thinking about a series of issues by writing a series of statements starting with "This I believe . . ." Their attitudes of the play of their children were then investigated by a structured interview in which parents were asked questions such as "Should boys play with dolls?" "Where in the house can the children play?" and "Can they use your tools?" Again it was possible to identify attitudes towards and the actual management of play that resulted in the placement of varying degrees of external constraint on the child's behavior.

The final link was forged by having the young children play with a laboratory playlike task that allowed the child's preferences for complexity, and for novel combinations to be displayed. The task was to select cardboard shapes varying in color and complexity, which were laid out in rows by color and columns by complexity, and arrange them as they wished them on a blank board. Measures like the child's willingness to break from the constraints of patterns and to deal with more complex shapes were assumed to be indicants of creativity or cognitive complexity.

As expected, the results of all three stages were consistent. Flexible mothers placed few constraints on the play of their children, providing a flexible and encouraging environment, and reared children who were more creative or flexible in their behavior. The fathers' influence on this process was minimal.

This study is cited because it is timely and illustrated precisely the principles that can be derived from the integrated concepts of play outlined in the previous chapter.

Children can be expected to play with whatever is arousing or wherever there are objects that provide arousing stimuli. Although there must be provision for play, space, and playthings, children will display a tendency to engage with the real and interesting objects in the home. The profusion of gadgets, tools, utensils, and ornaments are fertile sources of arousing stimuli. The child, even though he may have excellent toys in his own room, will want to play with the real things. This, with the obvious constraints required by the prevention of damage and injury, should be encouraged.

A further most important source of arousing stimuli are the other adults in the house. Events cluster about the busy adult. Naturally that is the best place to play. Sutton-Smith (1970) talks about this propensity to play under the adults' feet, in doorways and passages. This can be explained by attractiveness of the concentration of rewarding interaction with others, and the presumably ready access to the mothering-one. According to Bishop and Chace, some parents encourage and tolerate the flexible interaction of their children with their material goods, themselves, and activities. This is good and leads to a greater behavioral flexibility in their children.

To establish an appropriate environment for tiny children is difficult since their demands for attention are great, but this is because at this time they know least and are learning most rapidly. Neumann's criteria again suggest how to act. When children are attempting to acquire a required and defined response, they should be gently but firmly pressured into its production. When the children are at play, which is the time remaining after life-support activities are completed, they should be placed in situations where arousing engagements are possible. This means that children be allowed access to toys, appropriate artifacts in the home, and of course the most complex and interesting object in the house—the mothering-one.

The interactions with the environment, whether alone or in joint action with the mothering-one, should first be explored then investigated, manipulated, and then should lead on to epistemic behavior. Exploration and investigation as strategies for arousal generation were clearly defined by Berlyne (1960), who differentiated them and further subdivided them. Exploration involves the production of information concerning an object or situation by self-manipulation. Thus looking at something, orienting to it, then walking around it without acting upon it are exploratory behaviors. When the individual acts upon the object to determine its properties, i.e., what happens, then it is investigated. Investigation is in fact usually manipulation, although it might be that an investigator uses the manipulations of others to gain information. In the human case, at least, verbal communications can be manipulations in that they act upon and elicit responses from other humans.

These interactions can be enriched by the mothering-one if the nature of the playful process is understood. After the child has explored, there follows the investigation of the properties of an object with the child identifying the cause-effect relationships embedded in the object. At this stage the child needs to test the reliability of its hypotheses about what will happen given a response. The establishment of reliable effect predictions depends upon repetition. In the life of the very young child this repetition is especially apparent. The limiting constraints of the physical environment are tested. The child who drops items from the highchair can be thought of as making repeated tests of what happens when things are left unsupported in the air. They then disappear. After a while the child notices they fall and moves to the next question. Given the circumstances, do they always fall? This kind of experimentation takes many replications.

Once simple relationships have been established, they are complicated or made more complex. The antecedent conditions are varied, and the effects of given responses are retested. This kind of behavior is extended to all available objects in time, and also to other humans in the setting. The mothering-one can make sure that there are many responsive items within the child's reach, and she can add elements to complexify the setting as the child plays and learns.

Once a particular cause-effect relationship is learned, it can form the basis for more sophisticated interactions and be incorporated into symbols. Once symbols are present, epistemic behavior is possible and the possibilities for the child are broadened. When language is acquired, verbal incongruities, puns, rhymes, can then join the array of arousing events.

Once relationships have been replicated sufficiently to have produced highly reliable predictions as to outcomes, then the mother can create dissonance by exposing the child to the exceptions. For example, if all things fall when unsupported why does a helium balloon not fall. A host of interesting (novel, complex, or dissonant) interactions follow.

A child needs myriad interactions to maintain optimal arousal. Some homes provide these. These homes contain much varied material, kept there for use by both adults and children, and they are populated by adults who are willing to interact with the children, despite their other tasks. When to this is added a willingness to reduce constraints to the minimum, consistent with the preservation of life and material and the enculturation of the child, then the home will foster the escalation of the child's complexity and development. In homes where there is a paucity of material or cooperative adult-child interactions, where there are massive and rigid constraints on what responses are permissible, or where the behavior of the child is preempted by other prepotent needs, then play cannot develop. Soon the complexity of the child exceeds that of the environment, the available interactions are redundant and boring, and further development is slowed.

Morris (1964) after observing caged zoo animals, particularly primates, wrote down their strategies for dealing with boring situations.

He noted that in a restricted environment they:

1. introduce novelty themselves by inventing new motor patterns.
2. increase the complexity of their environment by performing acts that create stimulus situations to which they react.
3. increase the quality of their reactions to the normal stimuli that are available.
4. vary the quality of their reactions to normal stimuli that are available.
5. may perform normal responses to sub-normal situations.
6. emit stereotyped responses.

A moment's reflection reveals that children behave similarly to Morris' zoo animals under boring and restrictive circumstances. To an adult who either wishes to constrain a child directly, or has unwittingly structured an environment that is boring and contains a trapped child, all these classes of behavior may seem inappropriate. Children as they escalate their attempts to generate arousing interactions are seen to become progressively naughtier, and may ultimately be accused of "acting-out" behavior if they are driven to extremes.

Some homes may be boring if most of the interesting activities that exist naturally are proscribed and if there is no compensatory provision of other materials and actions. Similar circumstances exist outside the home per se, mostly where the environment or activity has been designed to exploit the capacity of the adult to tolerate inactivity by engaging in epistemic behavior by thinking, reading, daydreaming, etc. In situations requiring quiescence for long periods, the smaller capacity of young children to generate arousal from cognitive events faces them eventually with serious sensory deprivation. Their behavior while waiting or traveling exemplifies the strengths of the arousal-seeking drive. They brave the punishments of adults repeatedly in order to drive up the level of stimulation in their environment.

High-rise apartments, the places that many young families are now forced to call home, also necessarily constrain the opportunities of the child to indulge in the stimulation seeking of play. They are usually small, with little space available to contain the material chaos that results from the free play of children. They are designed for adults, with space for what adults do. Apartments require high density living and from this there follows a pressure to reduce the intensity of behavior so that others are not disturbed. Further, the space in which an apartment dwelling child may explore during his play time is sadly curtailed. Even though young children do not wish to roam far from their mother in most apartments, there is no natural progression by which the child may gradually increase the size of his territory. In apartments, the child has to move beyond the immediate threshold and in a very short distance he is in public space out of sight and control of the mothering-one. The physical removal of mother and playing child by the interposition of stairways, elevators, and access-ways, makes mothers reluctant to allow even their older children to wander far from the territory they control. Children whose mothers are reluctant to let them roam freely must play in the apartment, in the access-ways near the apartment, or when specially supervised by the mother outside the apartment. These limitations on the access to play of children of apartment dwellers are causing increasing concern, particularly in Europe.

Winter (1966) reports that apartment dwelling American children had significantly fewer playmates than children of families living in single family dwellings. Further, there were, as was to be expected, significant constraints on the use of space imposed by apartment dwelling parents that were not imposed by parents in single family dwellings. The European concern for the quality of life of young apartment dwellers seems to surface earlier than in America, and an entry into the European literature can be gained from Stewart (1970). As a result of high density, specialization, and replication of the housing units and the lack of collective control over the communal space due to the high traffic of strangers, serious questions are being raised concerning the impact of high-rise apartment dwellings on the lives of all who live there. The problem of providing an adequately enriched but safe environment for apartment children has not been solved.

The home life of the child and his play there is critical. As in the school, Neumann's criteria seem applicable, suggesting when the mothering-one should be concerned with facilitating work or play. Two major sources of variance among homes in their provisions for play have been identified. The attitudes of the mothering-one, leading to the disposition of human and material resources to allow for play, and the nature of the living arrangements themselves. Both can be improved by study of the nature of play and its motives.

Playthings

Children play with objects or playthings for the same reason they play with other children or their own motor and physical characteristics. Playthings provide a source of arousing interactions. The things children play with extend far beyond the limitations of the adult conception of a toy or a playground. Both toys and playgrounds are external provisions made by adults solely for the purpose of facilitating play in the child. As an outcome of having made these special provisions, many adults fall prey to the idea that children should only play with toys or playgrounds and feel justified in stopping children playing with real objects.

Play is a process of experiencing exploration, investigation, and manipulation and it leads eventually to thinking involving the integration of previous with current experiences or epistemic behavior. The broader the range of experiences achieved the better. If Neumann's criteria can be applied, and damage to people or materials is not likely, then the child should be allowed to engage in any interaction with its environment. In other words, within the constraints of human and property rights, children should be encouraged to interact with all facets of their situation. As many of the material objects as possible in the child's environment should become legitimate playthings, not merely their toys or playgrounds. Thus while making an effort to encourage play by actively providing playthings, adults should also encourage engagement with the other objects in the environment, proscribing only those interactions that are damaging.

There are two categories of things played with, toys and playgrounds on the one hand, and the materials existing for other purposes on the other. By definition this section is restricted to toys and playgrounds, since those are the artifacts specifically produced for play. By this definition, for example, the deliberate provision of non-toys for the purpose of play makes them playthings. Deliberate provision implies to some extent that the object is selected with the ultimate use of the toy or playground in mind, which then raises the issue, "What are good playthings?"

It is possible to derive some guidelines for the selection of a plaything from the three principles that form the core of the arousal-seeking model. The principles are:

1. children play for the stimulation they receive;
2. that that stimulation must contain elements of uncertainty (they are to some extent novel, complex, or dissonant); and
3. that the interactions producing the stimulation must rise in complexity with the accumulation of knowledge about or experience with the object (the extent to which the uncertainty concerning the object is reduced).

These principles complement the questions derived from Neumann's criteria. Neumann was concerned with eliminating obstacles to intrinsically motivated or playful behavior by attending to the constraints placed by others on the consequences of that behavior. The present concern is with the nature of the playthings. Thus good playthings should have attributes that tend to allow the kinds of responses emitted by a child seeking arousal.

In the same way that Neumann recognized that there could not be an entirely free setting for behavior, it is recognized that there clearly are limits on the degree to which any toy or playground can satisfy the requirements for play. Some provided playthings are better than others in that they sustain play longer, which means that they elicit a greater variety or complexity of responses. The arousal-seeking model suggests the attributes playthings should have if they are to have a higher probability of eliciting and sustaining play.

Determining whether a plaything has these attributes, without a long, drawn out, and expensive research or evaluation procedure requires the formation of subjective judgments. These judgments concerning which is the better playground or toy at the purchasing point, or which is the better element or ingredient at the design point, can be guided by a series of statements. These statements deal with the essential nature of the behavior that can be emitted by a child interacting with a plaything and can provide the basic questions necessary for selection. Thus they are organized to deal with exploration, investigation, manipulation, and epistemic behavior:

Better playthings provide novelty from the point of view of a particular child. The plaything has attributes that are to some extent outside the previous experience of the child thereby engendering *exploration* prior to actual engagement with it.

Better playthings possess sufficient complexity to require *investigation* of their physical properties. A plaything should puzzle the child sufficiently that it has to be handled, poked, pulled, and tested. If the purpose of each element in the plaything is immediately apparent to the child so that its physical properties are predictable prior to the child's engagement with it, then it is less of a plaything.

Better playthings are responsive. They must produce some effect that is under the control of the child. They are *manipulable*. The more effects produced by the child's manipulations of its physical nature discovered during the investigatory phase, the better.

Finally, the better plaything is the one that poses questions to be pondered by the child when not actually in process of physical engagement with it. Pondering problems raised by previous experiences without the attachment of external or terminal consequences was earlier called epistemic behavior. *Epistemic behavior* produces arousal from novel, complex, or dissonant cognitive events, and the excellent plaything must eventually lead to this kind of problem-solving behavior.

It can be expected that the first two stages in playing with a plaything will be passed rapidly. Novelty is rapidly reduced by exploration and investigation and the plaything must then engender a wide variety of manipulations and thinking if it is to engage a child for more than a brief period of time.

In addition, it seems quite appropriate to select toys that generate contact with the principles of the technology necessary for human existence. Toys allowing the child who is sufficiently skilled to construct objects that satisfy the last two statements are to be encouraged.

Playgrounds

Playgrounds are no more than a combination of large playthings placed together in one location. There is no reason that playgrounds have to be outside but the tradition that has imposed this unnecessary constraint is strong, and few playgrounds are built indoors. Tradition has also decreed that a playground be designed to provide opportunities for gross motor activity by simulating, in galvanized steel, some primitive jungle setting. If the statements about playthings are applied to the average traditional playground, it can be seen to be a travesty.

The children agree. Playgrounds are often deserted. Wade (1968), for example, studied playgrounds in Philadelphia and noted that the average visit time to a playground was 15 minutes, and that during times identified for peak usage the nonmanipulable items stood idle the large majority (89–98%) of the time. Again, Dee and Liebman (1970) showed that attendance at a playground was inversely related to the existence of other activities provided by a neighborhood among other factors. The arousal-seeking explanation for play suggests the answers. Playgrounds are not used because they do not provide pacer stimuli, or interactions with an environment that spiral upwards in complexity as the child revisits a playground. The principles and statements laid out above can be applied just as easily to playgrounds as to playthings.

Toys have evolved towards appropriate complexity by virtue of selective pressure by their consumers, the children. Despite the fact that toys are largely purchased by adults, children have had some influence on their selection and toys have slowly improved. Not so with playgrounds. There has been little evolution in the standard playground; this year's playgrounds look very similar to those of 50 years ago.

There seem to be several factors contributing to this. The most critical drag on the evolution of playgrounds has been the assumption that it is possible to sustain play over the early life of a child without there being any alteration in the play environment. The nature of play as arousal-seeking suggests that unless the playground changes, and in fact quite rapidly, it soon becomes redundant and boring. Once boring it cannot function as a plaything.

Related to this is the practical matter of maintenance. It has been assumed that it is possible to design and maintain a playground for its capital cost alone; a good playground is one requiring very little maintenance. However, play is a process of consuming information. In the process, materials and human resources are consumed, and if playgrounds are to continue to function most of them require continual modification.

Finally, it has only rarely been considered necessary to staff a playground with a leader who has the responsibility to guarantee the provision of appropriate raw materials, and to catalyze changes in the playground and its activities. While playground leadership is sometimes provided during the summer, the leaders are often drawn temporarily and untrained from the ranks of the summer unemployed and asked to administer programs on the conventional playgrounds. Since the only elements that can be manipulated by the leader in the playground are the children, the program has to rely almost exclusively on games and competitions rather than cooperations, with the danger that individuals and their play rarely surface.

There seem to be two classes of playgrounds. Some playgrounds are built as diversions to occupy the attention of children brought to a playground or trapped there by their parents once, or at least infrequently. The other kind of playground is one that is visited repeatedly by the same users. The former would be in parks outside town, in zoos, or near museums that are the object of special trips, and the latter are obviously neighborhood playgrounds.

The one-visit playground may function successfully as a distractor if it merely provides sufficient novelty to sustain interactions for an hour or so. Since every playground is different from others in its setting and arrangement it will be to some extent novel. However, the playground can be designed to emphasize exploration and investigation. The acme for this type of playground is Disneyland. Here the contents of the setting are arranged to allow exploration in a setting that is richly novel. The individual is aroused by the pressure of novelty and does not engage in anything but visual and auditory contact with the environment. Of course this gives rise to thinking and perhaps new knowledge, but it is not permissible for a child to investigate and manipulate the artifacts as he wishes on repeated visits. Thus this class of playground only needs to provide arousing opportunities over a short time.

The neighborhood playground has a quite different clientele. The children coming onto this kind of playground have typically been there many times. As designed now the standard playground cannot provide the appropriate interactions year in and year out during the development of the neighborhood children. The neighborhood playground should represent a conscious attempt to complexify the children's neighborhood environment so that there are opportunities to explore, investigate, manipulate, and engage in epistemic behavior. This will require a quite different approach. Currently, nearly all playgrounds seem to be designed to produce only the first effect, gently diverting the child to gross motor activity when there is nothing else to do. An understanding of the nature of play as represented by the principles for designing toys should allow playground designers to first differentiate the goals of the playgrounds and then plan more appropriately.

The adventure playground that has evolved in Europe since World War II (Bengtsson, 1970; Hurtwood, 1968) has proved successful. The concepts derived above are exhibited by adventure and junk playgrounds. They are interesting areas filled with bricks, lumber, dirt, scrap metal. Here are provided the tools, the materials, and the discrete leadership and supervision such that children can dig, build, change their environment and undertake cooperative projects that can last a whole summer. Such playgrounds are consumable. Each child can manipulate the playthings and produce effects on them. The setting is dynamic, changing as the various children add their own modifications. Cooperation in the management of material and the development of plans is necessary and projects can be progressively elaborated. In junk playgrounds, children use real materials to construct their own playthings and the play occurs during the process of their building as well as in their use.

Play with Others: Cooperation and Competition

Since the most complex and changeable objects in the play environment of children are other children, thought must be given to their involvement. It is a fact of life that we are crowded together with other people and interdependent with them. These facts impinge on the lives of children, and they must of necessity learn to cope with the constraints of the rights and existence of other children, while benefiting from the complexity they bring to a setting. Neumann's criteria show that the presence of others in a playful interaction requiring coaction, cooperation, or competition places external controls on the behavior of the individuals. To some extent control has passed to others, a situation which on the one hand reduces the freedom of action of the individual, but on the other increases the possibility of arousing interactions not available to the solitary individual.

Social interaction is a requirement for competitions where the reward or payoff if achieved by one competitor is denied to the others. In competition the protagonists act against one another for mutually exclusive ends. Little or no attention in the realm of the design and selection of playthings has been given to situations where children act together to produce payoffs that benefit all, or at least do not exclude the others from being paid off. There are simple devices that require coaction and cooperation but compared to the number designed to induce competitive situations, they are very few. Yet the play of a group of children rapidly passes from competition to cooperation. If a group of children engage in a specific competition, a hierarchy is very rapidly established and the group is then faced with the necessity for further arousal-seeking. They will frequently explore cooperatively for opportunities to produce mutual arousal. This notion that children's play, and probably adults' also, often moves beyond competition, is supported by Eifermann's (1971) study. She showed that by the fourth or fifth grade peak interest in rule-governed and competitive gaming had been reached. Beyond that level interest dropped steeply.

A competition must not have a predictable outcome if it is to remain arousing for all. When clear superiority is detectable the central element in the process of a competition—the uncertainty of the outcome—is lost. When the process itself is not rewarding then the procedures must be sustained by the end product; feelings of power, trophies, or money for the winners and social obligation to continue by the losers. These are extrinsic to the process. To the degree that competition is sustained by extrinsic pressures, it is not play. The corollary is that the most playlike situations occur when the end result is actually of no concern to the participants and where their concern is with the mutually arousing nature of the procedures. In situations where the outcome is of importance, the most playlike situation occurs when the probability of winning is equal for all competitors.

These are conditions necessary for competitive activity to move as far as possible towards the playful end of the play-work continuum. To the extent that competitive activity becomes extrinsically determined, then it falls outside the purview of this book. However, the contemporary American scene imposes competition and competitiveness to such an extent that there is cause for concern that behaving for the rewards attendant on the processes themselves rather than the outcomes is often preempted. In this sense competition and play are antithetical.

There is a tendency for those organizing recreation programs, inside and outside of school, to lose sight of the playful ingredient and substitute competition for cooperation. Competition is easier to manage. The process of striving for excellence relative to others is the logical extension of an activity for those who are relatively able in an activity. Thus when uncertainty or impact of an activity is reduced by a given level of proficiency, its impact can be extended by adding the uncertainty of competition with an evenly matched set of opponents. Thus competition may come at the end of the process of progressive elaboration of the complexity of an activity. Competitions themselves are elaborated into a hierarchy of progressively more difficult opponents till the one best competitor is finally known. However, competitions are frequently placed at the beginning of the process, thus eliminating a stage in which the actors cooperate for the purposes of playing with the activity together.

The little leagues for the sports substitute concern for the end rather than the process. The young children who participate should be cooperating to milk the sport-like setting of the interactions and uncertainties that are inherent in their activities. There is little need to force onto young children a clear resolution into a mutually exclusive outcome. The application of simplistic athletic models to the play of young children is inappropriate. When unfettered by league requirements the children gradually escalate the complexity of their interactions with a sport from playing with its techniques and constraints, through informal continuous and unresolved cooperative games, to low-grade competitions informally organized among themselves. Only after sixth grade, according to Eifermann (1971), would the need to escalate the complexity of these sandlot games make sense of leagues and formal competitions.

Current conceptions of competition are based on the assumptions that play and recreation inevitably are escalated in complexity and require competition. Eifermann's study flatly contradicts this, at least for a variety of settings and peoples in Israel. If this finding can be validated for the subcultures in other Western countries, the implications will require a major shift in attitude toward the role of competition in leisure.

Adult Play

Adults strive to arrange their lives so that Neumann's criteria apply to their activities at both work and play. This sounds paradoxical since Neumann established her criteria to discriminate working from playing. However, adults try to make their work playlike. The ideal job is recognized as one that one would do anyway. This is only a different way of saying that if the consequences of not working, the extrinsic rewards, were removed, the behavior would continue because of intrinsic motives. It is a commonly recognized fact that millionaires continue to play the game of their work, despite the fact that the impact of that work on the material quality of their lives is negligible.

Many people have arranged their lives so they are remunerated for what is intrinsically rewarding, and some are coming to see that the quantity of the extrinsic rewards (money and benefits) are beginning to lose their correlation with the length of preparation for that occupation and to begin to be related to the relative unpleasantness of the job. It is going to cost more as time goes on to persuade people to voluntarily submit to chronic sub-optimal arousal in boring repetitive occupations. In academic circles the grumbling jokes about the wages of plumbers, cement masons, auto-workers can be cut short by pointing out that lowly paid professors could change occupations. However, they prefer a situation where they can practice epistemic behavior and be rewarded both intrinsically and extrinsically by the process.

All recreations engaged in by people provide novel, complex, or dissonant interactions that generate arousing stimuli. When a recreational activity becomes sufficiently familiar, redundant, or simple then its attraction wanes and the individual will try to pass on to another activity. The course of engagements with leisure activities would seem to follow similar stages if the arousal-seeking model can provide the explanation. For the current case it is assumed that other motives to participate such as strong social pressures to conform or to affiliate with a group, etc., are not involved. While this assumption can rarely be met in reality, it is made here for the sake of clarity.

At the beginning, each activity involves novelty. The unfamiliarity of the task itself is sufficient to allow the elevation of arousal. As the task is learned then the uncertainty, and hence the impact of the activity, is maintained by the elevation of standards of performance. The probability of achievement of a goal response is maintained at some level so that the uncertainty of its achievement is optimally arousing to the individual. The establishment of the difficulty of the goal and likelihood of its achievement can usually be varied by the player and boils down to the levels of risk of success and failure the individual will take. Thus in order to maintain optimal arousal individuals will increase the difficulty of the task as their ability increases with learning. This behavior is only beginning to be studied from this point of view, but formerly was studied to build a theory of risk-taking. The behavior has been studied by personality psychologists but an additional factor, the individual need for uncertainty and arousal-seeking, should be included as a factor in the situation.

Once the activity has been learned to the extent that its mere practice fails to provide arousing stimulation, then it is elaborated. Artificial constraints on the activity or rules governing mode of achieving the performance are added. Then, in some cases, the activity is removed to a new setting or carried out with new people. Finally the process of complexification of the response is carried to the point where uncertainty in the outcome is dependent on the responses of others. An element of competition may be added. Here the outcome is determined by comparison with others and contains within the process the seeds of its own destruction. To the extent that the reward ceases to lie in the processes of interacting with an opponent and depends on the extrinsic reward of the goal, the activity becomes less playful. Competition can serve as a procedure whereby the processes themselves can be made uncertain by virtue of a complex code of rules governing the emission of difficult responses for the mutual enjoyment of the participants. Alternatively, it can serve as a struggle for a victory necessary for the psychic needs of the individual.

American adults seem confused about the purposes of games and competitions. This lack of understanding leads to failure to perceive that it is possible to play at games and work at games. However, to the extent that the gamelike activities indulged in by adults fail to satisfy Neumann's criteria, they fall outside the ambit of this book.

Increasing leisure means increasing periods during which our population is driven by their very nature to consume information. Many institutions in our society have their sustenance in the need for man to engage in arousing interactions with the environment, and Stephenson (1967) has developed the concept that the communications industry is really a leisure industry providing the raw material for epistemic behavior on the part of nearly all adults. The mass media—the press, radio, television, and publishing—plus the arts—art, theater, dance, creative writing—are the major adult-oriented manifestations of the need for a continually escalating complexity or novelty in cognitive events. The effort spent keeping up with the changing scene in the arts and current affairs is stimulus-seeking behavior driven by the optimal arousal model.

Apart from the communications industries and the arts as sources of stimulation, two other leisure institutions are organized to provide opportunities to engage in arousing activity. Adults expend effort to organize themselves into clubs or associations with others of like special interests. Considerable work is done to maintain the organization and it is rewarded by increased opportunity for engagement in a mutually complexified set of interactions that could not exist for the members independently. The other institution consists of the leisure service delivery systems that are organized either for profit or are tax-supported by the citizenry.

Professionally operated leisure service delivery systems are successful to the extent that they deliver opportunities for their patrons to engage in behavior that optimizes their arousal during nonworking hours. The public recreation professional and the private individual or organization providing leisure services must, to be successful, recognize why their patrons play. Principles for operation can be derived from that explanation.

There seem to be two major functions for those engaged in providing leisure services. They are the provision of face-to-face leadership and the provision of supervision and administration. These two areas of action can be sustained by the same view of leisure as a vital resource and of leisure behavior as motivated by many needs, a major one being the need to sustain arousal. These two sets of functions will be separated for the purposes of discussion only.

The face-to-face leader is charged with optimizing the interactions within a small group to realize the expectations of its members. One of the reasons people join the small group is their need for opportunities to deal with levels of information flow or impact that suits them at the time of joining. Usually such groups are initiated by recreation personnel as sources for instruction. Early participation is motivated not only by the anticipation of future leisure benefits, but also by the intrinsic uncertainty and challenge in acquiring a new skill.

There are dangers in relying on the capacity of future benefits to maintain practice, particularly in skills that are complex. This danger is of course that immediate gratification of the need for arousal is deferred or mortgaged for some presumed benefit later. While in an institutional setting, like a school, it is undesirable to deny the immediate in the search for eventual rewards, it may be necessary some of the time when specific necessary skills are sought. The school is charged by society with acculturating the individual. In leisure services the instructor is responsible not to society but to the individual.

Individual expectations are paramount. The participants should be able to expect a situation organized to allow them activities that are immediately arousing. The professional will clearly be called on to provide formal instruction in skills identified by the patrons as desirable. The process of their acquisition will be arousing and so long as there is uncertainty about the outcome, i.e., if there is a chance of further improvement, the activities will be arousing and desired. The face-to-face leader must be concerned with the elimination of extrinsic consequences and criteria as far as possible yet still produce individually satisfying progress towards greater skill. Therein lies the dilemma of recreators. At the same time, at least at the beginning of the process, they must instruct, but also must respect the individuality of their clients. Thus concern for objective improvement in performance must be balanced by the application of Neumann's criteria to the situation. The instruction and practice must be as playlike as possible commensurate with the desire of each individual to mortgage the present for the future, i.e., work rather than play.

Two simple principles can now be added to Neumann's criteria and applied to recreational instruction programs. First there will be differing requirements for attainment, and some clients will persist in the search for higher levels of performance. So there must be graded levels of instruction to allow a natural progression towards highly complex performance. Second, the professional then needs to plan an environment in which the skills acquired can be applied by each individual to progressively more complex situations.

The concern for individuality that faces the teacher also faces the recreator. The leader must be able to decide when the person is working at acquiring a skill and when a person is using the process of acquiring a skill as play. Simple assumptions that because a class has declared instructional bias it should have objective criteria for successful acquisition do not hold. Success must be evaluated in terms of the arousal-seeking behavior the activity sustains. Arousal-seeking requires novel, complex, and dissonant interactions. These interactions can only be related to an individual. Thus, success in a recreation setting can be gauged only in terms of an individual's expectations. In a recreation setting, as in education for creative problem-solving behavior, goals must be set for individuals rather than groups.

Individual goals may be quite separate from the declared objective of the class. Individuals may be interested in the skill itself and objective or competitive standards (competition determines success in terms of others' performance), they may be willing to swallow the pill of practice because of future opportunities, or they may see the class as a useful matrix of social interactions. In the first two situations the client is likely to be concerned with progress, but in the latter case criteria for successful participation are separated from the actual content of the class.

Catering creatively for a variety of possible outcomes and an increasing variance among members of the group is the hallmark of a good recreation leader and teacher. Cooperative interaction and a rejection of objective standards in favor of subjective ones are legitimate outcomes of leisure-time instruction.

After the termination of a series of classes the participants are usually more skillful and to differing degrees ready to utilize those skills at a higher level. If still finding the interactions surrounding the activity suitably arousing, clients will join another class designed to allow them to escalate their personal skills. Alternatively, they will seek to use their newly won skills in settings that either expose them to cooperative social activity, competition, or a mixture. The recreator's task is to facilitate this.

The best way to facilitate continuing interactivity by the client is to ensure that clubs of like-minded individuals and the facilities necessary to support their activities are available. This is because the capacity of man for complexity is enormous. It must be recognized that no professional recreator can operate at the highest level of sophistication necessary across more than a few activities. The goal must be to establish social systems in which like-minded clients are encouraged to act upon each other to provide the necessary complexity. Specialist clubs or associations are highly desirable and the recreation professional has the responsibility for providing facilities, initial instruction, and support to the leadership of special face-to-face interest groups. The existence of active clubs will allow like-minded clients to mutually escalate the complexity and variety of their engagements with the environment in the area of their special interest.

The emphasis of a leisure service delivery system must be in terms of the information flowing through the systems of its clients. The process of consuming leisure to produce optimal arousal is a dynamic one. The important ingredients of leisure are exploratory, investigative, manipulatory, and epistemic behaviors. These are active engagements with the environment that escalate in complexity. Passivity or repetition are anathema. The determination of success of any leisure service action must be made with regard to the kinds of behaviors it generates. The arousal-seeking model and Neumann's criteria would seem to provide the key.

Play and the Ill and Handicapped

Handicaps work a cruel double blow to the development of an individual. They limit the potential of the individual, and they handicap the processes whereby the person achieves his potential. The constraints of a handicap must be recognized, but because certain responses are denied the ill or handicapped individual does not mean that their need for arousal is lessened. With the exception of those whose arousal mechanisms are damaged, the need for play must be considered together with other needs.

Confinement of the ill or handicapped individual to bed for treatment or rest closely approximates the condition imposed by workers producing sensory deprivation. If the individual does not need sleep and is not sedated, then confinement rapidly leads to sensory deprivation which faces the individual with an additional problem. The provision of arousing events to the sick and handicapped is a responsibility of the hospital. It is a service made necessary by the inherent nature of the patient.

Nowhere are recreation services to the ill and handicapped needed more than in institutions delivering medical services to children and the developmentally retarded. Again, the lesser capacity of the children to engage in epistemic behavior, and the critical importance of play to their cognitive development, makes these services more critical. While short-term confinement may be tolerable by virtue of the novelty of the new setting, eventually as this becomes redundant the need for delivery of opportunities to continuously enter into arousing activity commences. This drive may not be strong if children are acutely ill, since their energies are preempted by the demands of their disease, but when they begin to recover or enter into a chronic phase where some of the energies are freed, their engagements with hospital environments soon become boring. Thus long-term confinement while ameliorating one condition may generate another.

Opportunities for arousal-seeking behavior are usually provided by activity, occupational, or recreational therapists. These workers are professionals involved in the patient as a whole who provide things for the patients to do within the constraints of their medical condition. It has been necessary for these professionals to justify their presence as members of the patient care team on the grounds that they intervene directly and influence the treatment of the patient's condition. While this may be the case on occasion when an activity is selected by the therapist on the grounds that its side effects beneficially influence the illness or handicap, in the majority of cases their provision of services does not have, nor does it need, a medical justification. Their job has only been questioned because of a puritanical attitude that considers play or arousal-seeking as trivial. If optimizing arousal is recognized as a basic human need, a need that maintains the engagement of the patients with their environments, then the provision of recreation services will become important in its own right as a human, not medical, service.

The ill and handicapped human have greater need for recreation or play services because their limited circumstances to some extent prevents their exploring for opportunities themselves. The principles for intervention to facilitate play in the ill and the handicapped are identical to those for delivering such services to the healthy. These require only an additional insight into the constraints imposed by the medical condition so that, where possible, the activities contribute to its remediation and, where they are not therapeutic, they do not hinder the effects of treatment.

Concluding Comment

Specific examples have deliberately been excluded from this chapter. The jump from the theoretical base to operational principles is as far as a theorist can go without prejudicing the generality of the arguments. The jump from general operational principles to specific behaviors in a given setting has to be the responsibility of the practitioner in that setting.

For the practitioner to make specific applications to a setting requires insights into explanations of cause and effect on behavior. The realm of play behavior is an enormous and complex one. It is important and therefore the responsibilities of those dealing with it are correspondingly great. Meeting these responsibilities can only come from a partnership between the objective knowledges of science and subjective knowledges of each practitioner. The links between these ways of knowing are provided by theories and principles. The intent of this chapter, and this book, was to make them available to both theoreticians and practitioners concerned with play.

REFERENCES

ALEXANDER, F. A contribution to a theory of play. *Psychoanalytic Quarterly,* 1958, 27, 175–193.

ANONYMOUS. *Encyclopaedia Brittanica,* 1968, 5, 72–73.

ANONYMOUS. Report to the President. White House Conference on Children. Washington, D.C.: U.S. Government Printing Office, 1970.

ASHBY, W. R. *Design for a brain: The origin of adaptive behavior* (2nd ed.). New York: John Wiley, 1960.

ATKINSON, J. W. Motivational determinants of risk-taking behavior. *Psychological Review,* 1957, 64, 359–372.

ATTNEAVE, F. *Application of information theory to psychology.* New York: Holt-Dryden, 1959.

AXLINE, V. M. Play therapy. Boston: Houghton-Mifflin, 1947.

BANKS, M. Personal communication, 1972.

BARKER, R. G. *One boy's day.* New York: Harper, 1951.

BARKER, R. G., & WRIGHT, M. F. *Midwest and its children.* New York: Harper & Row, 1955.

BARKER, R. G. *The stream of behavior: Explorations of its structure and content.* New York: Appleton-Cenutry-Crofts, 1963.

BARKER, R. G. *Ecological psychology.* Stanford: Stanford University Press, 1968.

BARNETT, S. A. *A study in behavior.* London: Methuen, 1963.

BEACH, F. A. Current concepts of play in animals. *American Naturalist,* 1945, 79, 523–541.

BEACH, F. A. The descent of instinct. In R. N. Haber (ed.), *Current research in motivation.* New York: Holt, Rinehart & Winston, 1966.

BENGTSSON, A. *Environmental planning for children's play.* New York: Praeger, 1970.

BENNETT, E. L., & ROSENZWEIG, M. R.   Brain chemistry and anatomy: Implications for theory of learning and memory. In C. Rupp (ed.), *Mind as a tissue.* New York: Harper & How, 1968. Pp. 63–86.

BERKOWITZ, L. A., & GREEN, J. A.   The stimulus qualities of the scapegoat. *Journal of Abnormal and Social Psychology,* 1962, 64, 293–301.

BERKOWITZ, L.   Aggressive cues in aggressive behavior and hostility catharsis. *Psychological Review,* 1964, 71, 104–122.

BERKOWITZ, L.   Simple view of aggression: An essay review. *American Scientist,* 1969, 57(3), 372–383.

BERKSON, G., & DAVENPORT, R. K., JR.   Stereotyped movements of mental defectives. I. Initial survey. *American Journal of Mental Deficiency,* 1962, 66, 849–852.

BERKSON, G., & MASON, W. A.   Stereotyped behaviors of chimpanzees; Relation to general arousal and alternative activities. *Perceptual and Motor Skills,* 1964, 19, 635–652.

BERKSON, G., MASON, W. A., & SAXON, S. V.   Situation and stimulus effects on stereotyped behaviors of chimpanzees. *Journal of Comparative Physiology,* 1963, 56, 786–792.

BERLYNE, D. E.   *Conflict, arousal and curiosity.* New York: McGraw-Hill, 1960.

BERLYNE, D. E.   Motivational problems raised by exploratory and epistemic behavior. In S. Koch (ed.), *Psychology as a science.* New York: McGraw-Hill, Vol. 5, 1963. Pp. 284–364.

BERLYNE, D. E.   Curiosity and exploration. *Science,* 1966, 153, 25–33.

BERLYNE, D. E.   Laughter, humor and play. In G. L. Lindzey and E. Aronson (eds.), *Handbook of social psychology.* New York: Addison-Wesley, 1968. Pp. 795–853.

BERNARD, L. L.   *Introduction to social psychology.* New York: Henry Holt & Co., 1926.

BERNSTEIN, N.   *The coordination and regulation of movements.* Oxford: Pergamon, 1967.

BISHOP, D. W., & CHACE, C. A.   Parental conceptual systems, home play environment, and potential creativity in children. *Journal of Experimental Child Phychology,* 1971, 12, 318–338.

BLOOM, B. S.   *Stability and change in human characteristics.* New York: Wiley, 1964.

BLURTON-JONES, N. G.   An ethological study of some aspects of social behavior of children in nursery school. In D. Norris (ed.), *Primate Ethology.* London: Weidenfeld & Nicolson, 1967. Pp. 347–368.

BLURTON-JONES, N. G.   Characteristics of ethological studies of human behavior. In N. G. Blurton-Jones (ed.), *Ethological studies of child behaviour.* Cambridge, England: Cambridge University Press, 1972. Pp. 3–33.

BLURTON-JONES, N. G.   Categories of child-child interaction. In N. G. Blurton-Jones (ed.), *Ethological studies of child behaviour.* Cambridge, England: Cambridge University Press, 1972. Pp. 97–127.

BLURTON-JONES, N. G.   Comparative aspects of mother-child contact. In N. G. Blurton-Jones (ed.), *Ethological studies of child behaviour.* Cambridge, England: Cambridge University Press, 1972. Pp. 305–327.

BLURTON-JONES, N. G.   Non-verbal communication in children. To appear in R. A. Hinde (ed.), *Non-verbal communication.* Cambridge, England: Cambridge University Press, in press.

BREER, P. E., & LOCKE, E. A.   *Task experience as a source of attitudes.* Homewood, Ill.: Dorsey Press, 1965.

BRONFENBRENNER, U.   Early deprivation in mammals: A cross species analysis. In G. Newton and S. Levine (eds.), *Early experience and behavior.* Springfield, Ill.: Charles C Thomas, 1968. Pp. 627–764.

BUCKNER, D. N., & MCGRATH, J. J. (eds.)   *Vigilance: A symposium.* New York: McGraw-Hill, 1963.

BURGERS, J. M.   Curiosity and play: Basic factors in the development of life. *Science,* 1966, 154, 1680–1681.

BUTLER, R. A.   Discrimination learning by rhesus monkeys to visual-exploration motivation. *Journal of Comparative and Physiological Psychology,* 1953, 46, 95–98.

BUTLER, R. A.   Exploratory and related behavior: A new trend in animal research. *Journal of Individual Psychology,* 1958, 14, 111–120.   (a)

BUTLER, R. A.   The differential effect of visual and auditory incentives on the performance of monkeys. *American Journal of Psychology,* 1958, 71, 591–593.   (b)

CANNON, W. B.   *The wisdom of the body.* New York: Norton, 1932.

CHERRY, C.   *On human communications; a review, a survey, and a criticism* (2nd ed.).   Cambridge, Mass.: M.I.T. Press, 1966.

COFER, C. N.   Motivation. *Annual Review of Psychology,* 1959, 10, 173–202.

DAVENPORT, R. K., JR., & BERKSON, G.   Stereotyped movements of mental defectives: II. Effects of novel objects. *American Journal of Mental Deficiency,* 1963, 67, 879–882.

DAVENPORT, R. K., & MENZEL, E. W., JR.   Stereotyped behavior of the infant chimpanzee. *Archives of General Psychiatry,* 1963, 8, 99–104.

DEE, N., & LIEBMAN, J. C.   A statistical study of attendance at urban playgrounds. *Journal of Leisure Research,* 1970, 2, 145–159.

DEMBER, W. N., & EARL, R. W.   Analysis of exploratory, manipulatory, and curiosity behaviors. *Psychological Review,* 1957, 64, 91–96.

DENNIS, W.   Infant development under conditions of restricted practice and of minimum social stimulation. *Genetic Psychological Monographs,* 1941, 23, 143–189.

DORFMAN, E.   Play therapy. In C. R. Rogers (ed.), *Client centered therapy.* Boston: Houghton-Mifflin, 1951. Pp. 235–277.

DUFFY, E.   The psychological significance of the concept of "arousal" or "activation." *The Psychological Review,* 1957, 64, 265–275.

EDWARDS, E. *Information transmission; an introductory guide to the application of the theory of information to the human sciences.* London: Chapman & Hall, 1969.

EIFERMANN, R. R. Social play in childhood. In R. E. Herron and B. Sutton-Smith (eds.), *Child's play.* New York: Wiley & Sons, 1971. Pp. 270–297.

ERIKSON, E. H. *Childhood and society.* New York: Norton, 1950.

ERIKSON, E. H. Growth and crises of the healthy personality. *Psychological Issues,* 1959, 1, 50–100.

ESCALONA, S. Play and substitute satisfaction. In R. G. Barker *et al.* (eds.), *Child behavior and development.* New York: McGraw-Hill, 1943. Pp. 363–378.

FESHBACH, S. The catharsis hypothesis and some consequences of interaction with aggressive and neutral play objects. *Journal of Personality,* 1956, 24, 449–462.

FISKE, D. W., & MADDI, S. A conceptual framework. In D. W. Fiske and S. Maddi (eds.), *Functions of varied experience.* Illinois: Dorsey Press, 1961. Pp. 11–56.

FLAVELL, J. H. *The developmental psychology of Jean Piaget.* Princeton, N.J.: Van Nostrand-Reinhold, 1963.

FRANKMANN, J. P., & ADAMS, J. A. Theories of vigilance. *Psychological Bulletin,* 1962, 59, 259–272.

FREEMAN, G. L. *The energetics of human behavior.* Ithaca, N.Y.: Cornell University Press, 1948.

FREUD, A. *The psycho-analytic treatment of children.* London: Imago, 1946.

FREUD, S. Beyond the pleasure principle. In J. Strachey (ed. and trans.), *The standard edition of the complete psychological works of S. Freud,* 1920–22, Vol. 18. London: Hogarth and the Institute of Psychoanalysis, 1955.

FREUD, S. Writers and daydreaming. In J. Strachey (ed. and trans.), *The standard edition of the complete psychological works of S. Freud,* 1906–1908, Vol. 9. London: Hogarth and the Institute of Psychoanalysis, 1959.

GESELL, A., & AMATRUDA, C. S. *Developmental diagnosis.* New York: Hoeker, 1941.

GEWIRTZ, J. L. The role of stimulation in models for child development. In C. A. Chandler, R. S. Lourie and A. D. Peters (eds.), *Early child care: The new perspectives.* New York: Atherton Press, 1968. Pp. 169–214.

GILMORE, J. B. Play: A special behavior. In R. N. Haber (ed.), *Current research in motivation.* New York: Holt, Rinehart & Winston, 1966. Pp. 343–355. (a)

GILMORE, J. B. The role of anxiety and cognitive factors in children's play behavior. *Child Development,* 1966, 37 397–416. (b)

GLASS, D. C. (ed.), *Environmental influences.* New York: Rockefeller University Press and Russell Sage Foundation, 1968.

GORDON, I. J. *Baby learning through baby play: A parents' guide for the first two years.* New York: St. Martin's, 1970.

GRAMZA, A. F.   Unpublished report.   Motor Performance and Play Research Laboratory, Children's Research Center, University of Illinois, 1970.

GRAY, S. W., & MILLER, J. O.   Early experience in relation to cognitive development. *Review of Educational Research: Growth, Development and Learning,* 1967, 37, 475–493.

GROOS, K.   *The play of animals* (trans. E. L. Baldwin).   New York: Appleton, 1898.

GROOS, K.   *The play of man* (trans. E. L. Baldwin from original publication in 1898).   New York: Appleton, 1901.

GROOS, K.   Das spiel als katharsis.   *Zeitschrift für Päd (ogologische) u. Ex. Päd.,* Dec. 7, 1908.   Cited by G. T. W. Patrick, The psychology of play.   *Journal of Genetic Psychology,* 1914, 21, 469–484.

GULICK, L.   Interest in relation to muscular exercise.   *American Physical Education Review,* 1902, 7, 57–65.

GULICK, L.   Some psychical aspects of physical exercise.   *Popular Science Monthly,* 1898, 58, 793–805.

GUMP, P. V., SCHOGGEN, P., & REDL, F.   The behavior of the same child in different milieus.   In R. G. Barker (ed.), *The stream of behavior.*   New York: Appleton-Century-Crofts, 1963.   Pp. 169–202.

HAGEDORN, R., & LABOWITZ, S.   Participation in community associations by occupation: A test of three theories.   *American Sociological Review,* 1968, 33, 272–283.

HALL, G. S.   *Adolescence: Its psychology and its relations to physiology, anthropology, sociology, sex, crime, religion and education,* Vol. I.   New York: Appleton, 1916.

HARLOW, H. F.   Learning and satiation of a response in intrinsically motivated complex puzzle performance by monkeys.   *Journal of Comparative Physiological Psychology,* 1950, 43, 289–294.

HARLOW, H. F.   Motivation as a factor in the acquisition of new responses.   In D. Levine (ed.), *Current theory and research in motivation: A symposium.*   Lincoln, Neb.: University of Nebraska Press, 1953.   Pp. 24–49.

HARLOW, H. F., HARLOW, M. K., & MEYER, D. R.   Learning motivated by a manipulation drive.   *Journal of Experimental Psychology,* 1950, 40, 228–234.

HEBB, D. O.   *The organization of behavior.*   New York: Wiley & Sons, 1966.

HEBB, D. O., & THOMPSON, W. R.   The social significance of animal studies.   In G. Lindzey (ed.), *Handbook of social psychology.*   Cambridge, Mass.: Addison-Wesley, 1954.   Pp. 532–561.

HEDIGER, H.   *Wild animals in captivity.*   London: Butterworths, 1950.

HENDRICK, I.   Instinct and ego during infancy.   *Psychoanalytic Quarterly,* 1942, 11, 33–58.

HINDE, R. A.   Energy models of motivation.   *Symposium of the Society for Experimental Biology,* 1960, 15, 199–213.

HINDE, R. A.   *Animal behavior: A synthesis of ethology and comparative psychology.*   New York: McGraw-Hill, 1966.

HOKANSON, J. E., & BURGESS, M.   The effects of three types of aggression on vascular processes. *Journal of Abnormal and Social Psychology*, 1962, 64, 446–449.

HOLLIS, J. H.   The effects of social and nonsocial stimuli on the behavior of profoundly retarded children. Part II. *American Journal of Mental Deficiency*, 1965, 69, 772–789.

HUIZINGA, J.   *Homo Ludens: A study of the play element in culture.*   New York: Routledge & Kegan Paul, 1949.

HULL, C. L.   *Principles of behavior.*   New York: Appleton-Century-Crofts, 1943.

HUNT, J. McV.   Intrinsic-motivation and its role in psychological development. In D. Levine (ed.), *Nebraska Symposium on Motivation.* Lincoln, Neb.: University of Nebraska Press, 1965. Pp. 189–282.

HURTWOOD, L. A. O.   *Planning for play.*   London: Thames & Hudson, 1968.

HUTT, C.   Exploration and play in children. In P. A. Jewell and C. Loizos (eds.), *Play, exploration and territory in mammals. Symposia of the Royal Zoological Society of London, #18.*   London: Academic Press, 1966. Pp. 61–79.

HUTT, C., and HUTT, S. J.   Effects of environmental complexity on stereotyped behavior of children. *Animal Behavior,* 1965, 13, 1–4.

JAMES, W.   *Principles of psychology.*   New York: Holt, 1890. (Republished: New York: Dover, 1950.)

JEANRENAUD, C. Y.   Play behavior of young children in a novel situation. Unpublished master's thesis, University of Illinois, 1969.

JONES, A.   Stimulus-seeking behavior. In J. P. Zubek (ed.), *Sensory deprivation: Fifteen years of research.*   New York: Appleton-Century-Crofts, 1969. Pp. 167–206.

KAGAN, J., & BERKUN, M.   The reward value of running activity. *Journal of Comparative and Physiological Psychology,* 1954, 47, 108.

KAUFMAN, M. E., & LEVITT, H.   A study of three stereotyped behaviors in instittutionalized mental defectives. *American Journal of Mental Deficiency,* 1965, 69, 467–473.

KELLY, G. A.   Man's construction of his alternatives. In G. Lindzey (ed.), *Assessment of human motives.*   New York: Rinehart, 1958. Pp. .33–64.

KENNY, D. T.   An experimental test of the catharsis theory of aggression. *Dissertation Abstracts,* 1953, 13, 441.

KERLINGER, F. N.   *Foundations of behavioral research.*   New York: Holt, Rinehart & Winston, 1967.

KIBLER, A. W.   The relevance of vigilance research to aerospace monitoring tasks. *Human Factors,* 1965, 7, 93–99.

KIMBLE, G. A.   *Hilgard and Marquis' conditioning and learning* (2nd ed.). New York: Appleton-Century-Crofts, 1961.

KLEIN, M.   Personification in the play of children (1929). In M. Klein (ed.),

Contributions to psychoanalysis. London: Hogarth Press and the Institute of Psychoanalysis, 1948. Pp. 215–226.

KLEIN, M. The psychoanalytic play-technique. *American Journal of Orthopsychiatry*, 1955, 25, 223–237.

KOCH, H. L. An analysis of certain forms of so-called "nervous habits" in young children. *Journal of Genetic Psychology*, 1935, 46, 139–170.

KOHLBERG, L. Early education: A cognitive-developmental view. *Child Development*, 1968, 39, 1013–1062.

KRAVITZ, H., ROSENTHAL, V., TEPLITZ, A., MURPHY, J. B., & LESSER, R. E. A study of head-banging in infants and children. *Diseases of the Nervous System*, 1960, 21, 203–208.

KRECH, D. Psychoneuro-bio-chem-education. *Phi Delta Kappan*, March, 1969. 370–375.

LEACH, G. M. A comparison of the social behavior of some normal and problem children. In N. G. Blurton-Jones (ed.), *Ethological studies of child behaviour.* Cambridge, England: Cambridge University Press, 1972. Pp. 249–281.

LEBO, D. The development of play as a form of therapy. From Rousseau to Rogers. *American Journal of Psychiatry*, 1955–56, 112, 418–422.

LEUBA, C. Toward some integration of learning theories: The concept of optimal stimulation. *Psychological Reports*, 1955, 1, 27–33.

LEVITT, H., & KAUFMAN, M. E. Sound induced drive and stereotyped behavior in mental defectives. *American Journal of Mental Deficiency*, 1965, 69, 729–734.

LEVY, D. M. On the problem of movement restraint. *American Journal of Orthopsychiatry*, 1944, 14, 644–671.

LEWIN, K. *Field theory in social science; selected theoretical papers* (1st ed.). D. Cartwright (ed.) New York: Harper, 1951.

LIEBERMAN, J. N. Playfulness: An attempt to conceptualize a quality of play and the player. Private publication from Brooklyn College of CUNY and presented in part at Eastern Psychological Association, New York, April, 1966.

LIEBERMAN, J. N. Playfulness and divergent thinking: An investigation of their relationship at the kindergarten level. *Journal of Genetic Psychology*, 1965, 107, 219–224.

LINDER, S. *The harried leisure class.* New York: Columbia University Press, 1970.

LINDSLEY, D. B. The ontogeny of pleasure: Neural and behavioral development. In R. G. Heath (ed.), *The role of pleasure in behavior.* New York: Harper & Row, 1964. Pp. 3–22.

LINFORD, A. G., & JEANRENAUD, C. Y. A behavioristic model for a four stage play theory. *Contemporary Psychology of Sport.* Chicago: The Athletic Institute, 1970. Pp. 447–450.

LOCKARD, R. B. Reflections on the fall of comparative psychology: Is there a message for us all? *American Psychologist*, 1971, 26, 168–179.

LOIZOS, C.   Play in mammals.   In P. A. Jewell and C. Loizos (eds.), *Play exploration and territory in mammals. Symposia of the Royal Zoological Society of London, #18.* London: Academic Press, 1966. Pp. 1–9.

LORE, R. K.   Activity-drive hypothesis: Effects of activity restriction. *Psychological Bulletin,* 1968, 70, 566–574.

LOURIE, R. S.   The role of rhythmic patterns in childhood. *American Journal of Psychiatry,* 1949, 105, 653–660.

LOVELACE, G.   Responses of educable mentally handicapped and normal children to a unique plaything.   Unpublished master's thesis, University of Illinois, 1971.

MACKWORTH, J.   *Vigilance and attention.*   Baltimore, Md.: Penguin, 1970.

MACKWORTH, N. H.   Researches on the measurement of human performance. *Medical Research Council Special Report Service,* 1950, 268.   Cited by H. W. Sinaiko (ed.) *Seelcted papers on human factors in the design and use of control systems.*   New York: Dover Publications, 1961.

MAIER, H. W.   *Three theories of child development.*   New York: Harper & Row, 1965.

MALLICK, S. K., & McCANDLESS, B. R.   A study of catharsis of aggression. *Journal of Personality and Social Psychology,* 1966, 4, 591–596.

MALMO, R. B.   Activation: A neuro-psychological dimension. *Psychological Review,* 1959, 66, 367–386.

MASON, W. A.   Early deprivation in biological perspective.   In V. H. Denenberg (ed.), *Education of the infant and young child.*   New York: Academic Press, 1971. Pp. 25–50.

McDOUGALL, W.   *Outline of psychology.*   New York: Scribner's & Sons, 1923.

MENNINGER, W. C.   Recreation and mental health.   In B. Hill (ed.), *Recreation and psychiatry.*   New York: National Recreation Association, 1960. Pp. 8–18.

MENZEL, E. W., DAVENPORT, R. K., JR., & ROGERS, C. M.   Effects of environmental restriction upon the chimpanzee's responsiveness in novel situations. *Journal of Comparative Physiological Psychology,* 1963, 56, 329–334.

MESSER, S. B., & LEWIS, M.   Social class and sex differences in the attachment and play behavior of the year old infant. *Research Bulletin of ETS Princeton, N.J.,* February, 1970.

MILLAR, S.   *The psychology of play.*   Baltimore: Penguin, 1968.

MILLER, G. A., GALANTER, E., & PRIBRAM, K. R.   *Plans and the structure of behavior.*   New York: Holt, Rinehart & Winston, 1960.

MILLER, J. G.   Input overload and psychopathology. *American Journal of Psychiatry,* 1960, 116, 695–704.

MONTGOMERY, K. C.   The effect of hunger and thirst drives upon exploratory behavior. *Journal of Comparative and Physiological Psychology,* 1953, 46, 315–319.

MONTGOMERY, K. C.   The role of exploratory drive in learning. *Journal of Comparative and Physiological Psychology,* 1954, 47, 60–64.

MORRIS, D.   Occupational therapy for captive animals.   *Collected papers of the Laboratory Animal Center,* 1962, 11, 37–42.

MORRIS, D.   The response of animals to a restricted environment.   *Symposium of the Zoological Society of London,* 1964, 13, 99–118.

MORRIS, D.   *The human zoo.*   New York: McGraw-Hill, 1969.

MOUSTAKAS, C. E.   *Psychotherapy with children.*   New York: Harper & Bros., 1959.

NEUMANN, E. A.   The elements of play.   Unpublished doctoral dissertation, University of Illinois, 1971.

NIGHSWANDER, J. K., & MEYER, G. R.   Catharsis: A means of reducing elementary school students' aggressive behavior.   *Personnel and Guidance Journal,* 1969, 47, 461–465.

NISSEN, H. W.   A study of exploratory behavior of the white rat by means of the obstruction method.   *Journal of Genetic Psychology,* 1930, 37, 361–376.

NISSEN, H. W.   The nature of the drive as innate determinant of behavioral organization.   In M. R. Jones (ed.), *Nebraska symposium on motivation.* Vol. 2. Lincoln, Neb.: University of Nebraska Press, 1954. Pp. 281–320.

OLSON, W. C.   *The measurement of nervous habits in normal children.*   Minneapolis: University of Minnesota Press, 1929.

PAINTER, G. B.   *Infant education.*   San Rafael, Calif.: Dimensions, 1968.

PAINTER, G. B.   *Teach your baby; a complete tested program of simple daily activities for infants and small children designed to develop learning abilities to the fullest potential.*   New York: Simon & Schuster, 1971.

PATRICK, G. T. W.   The psychology of play.   *Journal of Genetic Psychology,* 1914, 21, 469–484.

PATRICK, G. T. W.   *The psychology of relaxation.*   Boston: Houghton-Mifflin, 1916.

PAVLOV, I. P.   Conditioned reflexes.   (Trans. G. V. Anrep).   Oxford: Clarendon Press, 1927.

PIAGET, J.   *Play, dreams and imitation in childhood* (trans. G. Gattegno and F. M. Hodgson).   New York: Norton, 1962. London: Routledge & Kegan Paul Ltd., 1951, reissued 1962.

PIAGET, J.   Response to Brian Sutton-Smith.   *Psychological Review,* 1966, 73, 111–112.

POOLE, T. B.   Aggressive play in polecats.   In P. A. Jewell and C. Loizos (eds.), *Play exploration and territory in mammals. Symposia of the Royal Zoological Society of London, #18.*   London: Academic Press, 1966. Pp. 23–38.

POPPER, K. R.   *The logic of scientific discovery.*   New York: Science Editions, 1961.

RAGHEB, M.   An integration of the theories of play.   Unpublished personal communication, 1971.

ROBERTS, J. M., & SUTTON-SMITH, B.   Game training and game involvement. *Ethnology,* 1962, 1, 166–185.

ROBERTS, J. M., SUTTON-SMITH, B., & KENDON, A.   Strategy in games and folk-tales.   *Journal of Social Psychology,* 1963, 61, 185–199.

SACKETT, G. P.   Effects of rearing conditions upon the behavior of rhesus monkeys (macaca mulatta).   *Child Development,* 1965, 36, 855–866.

SAMUELS, I.   Reticular mechanisms and behavior.   *Psychological Bulletin,* 1959, 56, 1–25.

SAPORA, A. V., & MITCHELL, E. D.   *The theory of play and recreation*   (3rd ed.).   New York: Ronald Press, 1961.

SARGENT, R. D., & KEIPER, R. R.   Stereotypies in caged canaries.   *Animal Behavior,* 1967, 15, 62–66.

SCHLOSBERG, H.   The concept of play.   *Psychological Review,* 1947, 54, 229–231.

SCHULMAN, J. L., KASPAR, J. C., & THRONE, F. M.   *Brain-damage and behavior: A clinical experimental study.*   Springfield, Ill.: Charles C Thomas, 1965.

SCHULTZ, D. D.   *Sensory restriction: Effects on behavior.*   New York: Academic Press, 1965.

SELYE, H.   *The stress of life.*   New York: McGraw-Hill, 1956.

SPENCER, H.   *Principles of psychology.*   Vol. 2, part 2 (3rd ed.).   New York: Appleton, 1896.

STEINMAN, W. M.   Is free play free?   *Educational Products Information Exchange Institute (EPIE) Product Report: Playground Equipment,* 3, #8 & 9, 6–8, 1970.

STEPHENSON, W.   *The play theory of mass communication.*   Chicago: University of Chicago Press, 1967.

STEWART, W. F. R.   *Children in flats: A family study.*   London: National Society for Prevention of Cruelty to Children, 1, Riding House St., London W1 8AA, 1970.

SUEDFELD, P.   Theoretical formulations: II.   In J. P. Zubek (ed.), *Sensory deprivation: Fifteen years of research.*   New York: Appleton-Century-Crofts, 1969.   Pp. 433–448.

SUTTON-SMITH, B.   The meeting of Maori and European cultures and its effects upon the unorganized games of Maori children.   *The Journal of the Polynesian Society,* 1951, 60, 93–107.

SUTTON-SMITH, B.   Play preference and play behavior: A validity study.   *Psychological Reports,* 1965, 16, 65–66.

SUTTON-SMITH, B.   Piaget on play: A critique.   *Psychological Review,* 1966, 73, 104–110.

SUTTON-SMITH, B.   A psychologist looks at playgrounds.   *Educational Products Information Institute (EPIE) Product Report: Playground Equipment,* 3, #8 & 9, 13–15, 1970.

SUTTON-SMITH, B., ROBERTS, J. M., & KOZELKA, R. M.   Game involvement in adults.   *Journal of Social Psychology,* 1963, 60, 15–30.

SUTTON-SMITH, B., ROSENBERG, B. G., & MORGAN, J. E. F.   Development of sex differences in play choices during adolescence. *Child Development,* 1963, 34, 119–126.

THOMPSON, W. R., & SCHAEFER, T., JR. Early environmental stimulation. In D. W. Fiske and S. R. Maddi (eds.) , *Functions of Varied Experience,* Homewood, Ill.: Dorsey Press, 1961. Pp. 81–105.

TOLMAN, E. C. *Purposive behavior in animals and men.* New York: Century, 1932. (Republished: New York, Meredith, 1967.)

WADDINGTON, C. A. (ed.) *Symposium on theoretical biology.* Vol. 1. London: Aldine, 1968.

WADE, G. R. A study of free play patterns of elementary school age children on playground equipment. Unpublished master's thesis, Pennsylvania State University, 1968.

WADE, M. G., ELLIS, M. J., & BOHRER, R. E. Biorhythms in the activity of children during free play. Unpublished paper, 1971.

WÄLDER, R. The psychoanalytic theory of play. *Psychoanalytic Quarterly,* 1933, 2, 208–224.

WEIKART, D. P., & LAMBIE, D. Z. Early enrichment in infants. In V. H. Denenberg (ed.) , *Education of the infant and young child.* New York: Academic Press, 1970. Pp. 83–107.

WELKER, W. I. An analysis of exploratory and play behavior in animals. In D. W. Fiske and S. Maddi (eds.) , *Functions of varied experience.* Homewood, Ill.: Dorsey Press, 1961. Pp. 175–226.

WHITE, R. W. Motivation reconsidered: The concept of competence. *Psychological Review,* 1959, 66, 297–333.

WINTER, M. Apartments and single family dwellings as they affect the play activities of preschool children. Unpublished master's thesis, Pennsylvania State University, 1966.

WITT, P. A., & BISHOP, D. W. Situational antecedents to leisure behavior. *Journal of Leisure Research,* 1970, 2, 64–77.

WITTY, P. A., & BEAMAN, F. N. The play of mental deviates. *Mental Hygiene,* 1933, 17, 618–634.

WOLF, R. M. The identification and measurement of environmental process variables related to intelligence. Unpublished doctoral dissertation, University of Chicago, 1964.

WOODWORTH, R. S. *Psychology: A study of mental life.* New York: Henry Holt, 1921.

WOODWORTH, R. S. *The dynamics of behavior.* New York: Holt, 1958.

YERKES, R. M., & DODSON, J. D. The relation of strength of stimulus to rapidity of habit formation. *Journal of Comparative Neurological Psychology,* 1908, 18, 459–482.

ZIPF, G. K. *Human behavior and the principle of least effort.* Cambridge, Mass.: Addison-Wesley, 1949.

ZUBEK, J. P.   Effects of prolonged sensory and perceptual deprivation.   *British Medical Bulletin,* 1964, 20, 38–42.

ZUBEK, J. P. (ed.)   *Sensory deprivation: Fifteen years of research.*   New York: Appleton-Century-Crofts, 1969.

ZUCKERMAN, M.   Theoretical formulations: I.   In J. P. Zubek (ed.), *Sensory deprivation: Fifteen years of research.*   New York: Appleton-Century-Crofts, 1969.   Pp. 407–432.

SUBJECT INDEX

Accomodation, 65-68, 125
  assimilation and, 61
  imitation and, 65
  intelligence and, 66-68
  reality and, 65-66
Achievement orientation, 72
Acting-out behavior, 133
Activation (see Arousal)
Activity, 76
  rats, 101
Activity drive, 32 (see Surplus energy)
Adult play (see also Play, Leisure)
  arousal levels and, 142
  Neumann's criteria and, 141-43
  recreation as, 142
  work and, 141-42
Aesthetic hunger, 27 (see also Instinct)
Aggression, 73 (see also Catharsis)
  anger and, 57
  catharsis and, 57
  frustration and, 57
  hostility and, 55-57
  play and, 54-57
Aggressive play, 18
Anxiety, 62, 63, 73
Appetitive behavior, 93
Approach/avoidance conflict, 97
  conflict, 97
Aristotle, 54
Arousal, 80-112, 86, 87, 89, 95 (see also
    Arousal level)
  behavioral effects of, 105
  behaviors producing, 96-99
  cognitive events and, 95
  drive to optimize, 93-96
  electrical activity in brain and, 105

Arousal (cont.)
  elevation of, toy play, 107
  epistemic behavior and, 90
  fun and, 100
  learning and, 94, 97
  novelty and, 92
  optimal level of, 91, 97, 107-8, 109, 115-
    18, 132
  performance and, 89-90, 107
  physiology of, 84, 89
  reinforcement and, 91
  sub-optimal levels of, 80-81, 87, 91
  supra-optimal levels of, 80-81, 90-91, 93,
    107-8
  uncertainty and, 93
Arousal level, 86 (see also Arousal)
  chronic sub-optimal, 104
  chronic supra-optimal, 105
  complexity and, 86
  incongruity and, 86
  novelty and, 86
  optimisation of, 104
  predictability and, 86
  reinforcement and, 91
  task difficulty and, 107
Arousal potential (see Impact)
Arousal seeking:
  hypothesis testing as, 103
  naughtiness as, 133
  play as, 118
  repetitious responding and, 102-4
Arousal-seeking model:
  principles of, 135
Arousal-seeking theory:
  reinforcers inherent, 117

161

Arousal seeking versus competence/effectance as a motive, 102
Arousing stimuli, 90
Arts:
  arousal seeking and the, 143
A/S ratio, 94 (see also Brain)
Assimilation, 61, 65-68, 125
  accomodation and, 61
  catharsis and, 61
  intelligence and, 66-68
  play and, 65-67
  unpleasant experiences, 60-61 (see also Catharsis, Cognitive theories of play, Play therapy)
Associations (see Clubs)
Attention, 84, 97, 106
  selective, 91
  uncertainty and, 93
Avoidance, 97
  approach versus, 97

Baseball, 43
Behavioral flexibility, 82, 94, 113-14 (see also Creativity)
  creativity and, 127
Behavioral variability, 116
Behavior modification, 25
Behavior primacy, 88, 103
Binary digit, 92
Biorhythms, 32-33
BIT, 92
Boredom, 80, 104, 133
  naughtiness, 133
  response to, 133
Brain, 82, 114
  A/S ratio in, 82
  association areas of, 82
  central processes in, 82
  cerebral cortex, 89-90
    inhibiting function of, 89-90
    interaction of reticulate arousal system and, 89
  efferent pathways, 89
  electrical activity and, 105
  epistemic behavior, arousal and, 90
  I/E ratio in, 82
  neural traffic in, 82
  reticulate arousal system, 86-90
    ablation of, 89
    arousal function of, 89-90
    cerebral cortex and, 89-90
  sensory-motor area of, 82
Breuer, 61

Catharsis, 59-60 (see also Cathartic theory, and Play therapy)

Catharsis (cont.)
  assimilation and, 61
  definition of, 55
Cathartic theory of play, 49, 52, 54-57, 62, 78
  compensation, 54
  relaxation and, 54
Causation, 25
Chance, games of, 72-74
Change:
  play and environmental, 114-18
  preparation for, 114
Children and work, 34
Classical theories of play, 23-47
  characteristics of, 23-24
  instinct theory, 23, 36-40, 46
  preparation theory, 23, 40-42, 47
  recapitulation theory, 23, 42-45, 47
  relaxation theory, 23, 33-36, 47
  surplus energy, 23, 27-33, 46
Clubs:
  arousing function of, 143
  function of, 145
  leisure services relation to, 145-46
Cognition, 64-70
  development and, 64, 118
  experience and, 64
Cognitive behavior, 99
Cognitive dynamic theory of play, 49-50, 79
Cognitive events, 90, 135
  arousing effect of, 90
Cognitive schemata, 64-67
  changing complexity of, 65
Collative variables, 100
Compensation theory of play, 49-54 (see also Cathartic and Psychoanalytic theories)
  catharsis, 54
  children, 53
  relaxation, 54
Competence/effectance theory of play, 30-31, 58, 100-104
  definition of, 102
  exploration and, 101
  manipulation and, 100
  mastery and, 102
  need reduction, 101
  reinforcement, effectance as, 102
Competition, 44, 55, 68, 74, 75, 138
  age preferences for, 140
  arousal and, 140
  catharsis and, 55
  difficulty of, 140-41
  games of, 68-69
  negative effects of, 139-41
  play versus, 141
  sports as, 141

Complexity, 86, 91, 98, 106, 115, 129, 130, 132, 144, 145
  definition of, 92
  environmental, 95-96
  individual nature, 95-96, 126
  information and, 92
  organism/environment interaction and, 104, 133
Confinement to bed as perceptual deprivation, 146-47
Conflict, 106 (see also Dissonance)
Conflict-enculturation hypothesis, 72-75
Consequences, 116 (see Reinforcement and Contingencies)
Consummatory act, 93, 101
Contingencies, 2, 5-6, 9, 25, 40, 70, 76, 107, 125
Cooperation, 138
  recreation programs and, 145
Cortico-reticular system (see Brain, Reticulate arousal system, and Cortex)
Covert play (see Epistemic behavior)
Creativity, 20, 121
Culture, 71-72, 116
  games and, 71-72
Curiosity, 84
  instinct for, 84-85

Day-care, 4
Daydreams, 123
Decentralization of sensory input, 108
Defence, 114
  direct, 114
  indirect, 115
  learning of, 115
  play and, 115-16
Definition of:
  aggression, inappropriate, 56
  aggression, thematic, 56
  catharsis, 55
  competence/effectance motive, 102
  complexity, 92
  epistemic behavior, 99
  exploration, 97-98
  homeorhesis, 96
  homeostasis, 96
  impact, 89
  information, 102
  instinct, 23, 36
  intrinsic motivation to play, 16-17
  investigation, 98
  neophilia, 81
  neophobia, 81
  pacer stimuli, 95-96
  play, 2, 9-22, 108-10
    as "just play," 9
    as undefinable, 12

Definition of (cont.)
  play (cont.)
    by three methods, 9-10
    common parlance, 9
    content, 9, 17-20
    motive, 9, 12-17
   criteria for, 12
  play therapy, 61
  plaything, 135
  process variable, 129
  reinforcement, 58
  sensoristasis, 93
  status variables, 129
  theory, 24
  work, 34, 110
Deprivation (see Environmental, Perceptual, Sensory, and Response deprivation)
Development:
  cognitive, 128
  complexity in children, 132
  inheritance/experience interaction, 117-18
  intelligence, 127
  Developmental stages in children, 65
Developmental theory of play, 79 (see Cognitive dynamic theory of play)
Dewey, 14
Discrimination of stimuli, 107
Dissonance, 91, 92, 106, 115, 129, 144, 145
  expectancy, 84-85, 86, 92
  incongruity as, 84-85
  individual nature of, 126
  puns, 132
  rhymes, 132
Divergent thinking, 21 (see also Creativity and Behavioral flexibility)
Drive:
  characteristics of, 93
Dwelling (see Home, High-rise apartments)

Education, 144
  acculturation function, 144
  creativity, 126-27
  goals, 120
  individual differences and, 121-27
  learning, 120
  play and, 4, 120-27
  recreation and, 120
  specific skills, 144
  utilitarian nature of, 120
Ego, 58
Emile, 4
Emotional release, 54, 57 (see also Cathartic, Compensation, and Relaxation theories of play)

Entertainment, 32-33
  arousal and, 143
Environmental deprivation, 101, 127-28
  hospitals and, 146-47
Environmental change, 82
  flexibility of behavior and, 82
Environmental enrichment, 128-29, 130, 134
Epistemic behavior, 99-100, 123, 131, 132
  (see also Cognitive events and Cognitive behaviors)
  arousal and, 95
  capability of adults/children, 133
  definition, 99
  etymological origin of, 99
  examples of, 99
  jokes as, 132
  laughter and, 99, 100
  playthings and, 136
  puns, 132
  rhymes, 132
  smiling, 100
  young children and, 100
Error, 107, 122
  creativity and, 122
  information content, 106
Ethology, 17
Etymology of play, 10
Evaluation, 28, 42
Excitability (see Response threshold)
Exercise primacy, 88
Expectancy, 84-85, 86, 92 (see also Dissonance)
Explanation (see Theory, function of)
Exploration, 80, 85, 97, 116, 131, 132, 135
  arousal and, 131
  change and, 83
  competence motive and, 100
  definition of, 97
  diversive exploration, 97
  drive for, 88
  locomotor, 97
  novelty and, 101
  playthings and, 136
  rats, 87-88
  specific exploration, 97
Extrinsic motive, 15 (see also Primary drives)
  elimination of, 16, 87-89, 121-27

Familiarity (see Novelty)
Fantasy, 60
Fatigue, 27, 28, 33, 35, 81
Fighting, 18, 55
  play fighting, discrimination of, 18
Filtering, 107

Flexibility of behavior, 82, 94, 113-14 (see also Creativity)
  evolution of, 82
Free play, 3
Free-range, 32, 134
Frustration (see also Catharsis)
  aggression and, 57
  work and, 51-54
Fun, 100

Games, 72-74
  competitive, 68-69, 74
  play and, 75
  recapitulation and, 43-44
  rule-oriented, 68-69
Generalisation theory of play, 49-54, 78
  (see also Learning theory of play)
  children, 53
Genotype, 113, 117

Habitat, 82
Habituation, 89
Handicap, 146-47
  arousal and, 147
  effects on development, 146
  play and, 146-47
Head start, 4
High-rise apartments:
  free-range of children in, 134
  play, effect on, 133
  proximity of child to mothering one, 134
Home environment, 127-34
  creativity and, 130
  materials provisions for play, 130-34
  play in, 127-34
Homeorhesis, 96
  definition of, 96
Homeostasis, 33, 96
  definition of, 96
Hospitalized children, 62
Hospitals:
  activity therapy in, 147
  children in, 62
  deprived environments, 146-47
  patients arousal in, 147
Hostility, 55 (see Cathartic theory of play)
  aggression and, 55
Humor, 69
  epistemic behavior as, 99
  overt responses of, 100
  ingredients of, 100
Hyperactivity, 32

Id, 58
Imitation, 41, 65 (see also Learning)
Impact, 89, 91-93, 96-97, 129
  definition of, 89
Inappropriate aggression, 56 (see also Aggression)
Incongruity, 84-86 (see also Dissonance)
Individual differences, 1 (see also Intra-specific differences)
  learning and, 121, 122
Information, 84-85, 104
  BIT as measure of, 92
  definition of, 102
  epistemic behavior and, 99
  load, 94, 129
  overload and its effects, 107-8
  quantification of, 92
  responses as, 92
  stimuli as, 92
Inheritance/experience interaction, 113-14, 117-18
Instinct, 15, 23, 40, 44, 64-65
  imitation and, 40-41
  inheritance of, 39-41, 42
  learning versus, 70
  man and, 37, 38, 39
  McDougall's list of, 37
  neurological basis of, 39
  surplus energy and, 38
Intelligence, 127
  play and, 65-67
Inter-specific differences, 113
Intra-specific differences, 113
  human, 121
    education and, 145
    recreation and, 145
Intrinsic motive (see also Play, as voluntary behavior)
  definition, 16
  differentiation from extrinsic motivation, 15-16
  play and, 15
Intrinsic reward, 14-15
Investigation, 97-98, 116, 131, 132, 135, 136
  arousal and, 131
  definition of, 98
  playthings and, 136
Investigatory reflex (see Orienting reflex)

Knowledge seeking (see Epistemic behavior)

Laughter (see Epistemic behavior)
  causes of, 100
Law of effect, 4, 58, 70

Lazarus, 14, 33
Learning, 4, 51, 58, 94, 101, 117
  acquired drives and, 5
  arousal and, 91, 97
  behavior modification, 5-6, 25
  cause/effect relations, 103
  culture and, 71-72
  education and, 120
  individual differences, 121
  instinct versus, 70
  law of effect, 4, 58, 70
  novel response emission, 113-15
  play and, 70
  primary drives, 5
  probabilistic outcomes, 103-4
  process versus status variables and, 129
  recreation and, 120
  specific responses, 120-22
  theory of, 70-71
  uncertainty and arousal in, 144
Learning theory of play, 50, 70-76, 79
  integrated with arousal and developmental theories, 112-18
Leisure:
  adults, 3
  antecedent experiences and, 52
  children's, 3
  education and, 51
  efficient use of, 3
  exploitation of children's, 4
  immediate versus deferred gratification in, 144
  leaving in, 144-45
  participation during, 51
  preferences in, 51
  resources for, 2
  specific skills necessary, 144
  work and, 49, 50-54, 142
  workers and, 50-54
Leisure activities:
  intrinsic motives for, 144
Leisure services:
  administrative support of clubs, 144
  arousal of clientelle, 149
  function of, 143
  leadership, 144
  Neumann's criteria and, 144
Locus of control:
  play and, 123

Management of play, 4, 147-48
Manipulation, 76, 80, 85, 87, 100-102, 116, 135
  change and, 83
  drive for, 88
  playthings and, 136

Mass media:
  arousal seeking and the, 143
  cognitive events and, 143
Mastery, 102 (see also Competence/effectance)
Mental retardation, 32
Motivation:
  intrinsic, 5, 120
  extrinsic, 5, 120

Naughtiness, 133
  response to boredom, 133
Need reduction, 85 (see also Primary drives)
Neophilia, 81-84, 109, 114
  definition, 81
  incessant activity and, 83
  novel responses and, 83
Neophobia, 40, 81-82
  definition of, 81
Neumann's criteria, 123-27, 134, 135, 144
Novel responses:
  positive and negative consequences and, 114
Novel toys, 63
Novelty, 63, 86, 90, 91, 97, 106, 115, 129, 130, 132, 144, 145
  absolute, 91, 92
  arousal created by, 92
  individual reference point and, 96, 126
  preference for intermediate levels of, 92
  relative, 91

Occupational role and leisure, 51
Ontogeny, 42 (see also Development)
Optimal arousal, 80-91
Orienting reflex, 83-84, 97 (see also Attention)

Pacers, 95-96, 106, 117, 129 (see also Complexity, individual nature of)
  definition of, 96
Pangburn, 14
Perception, 91
Perceptual deprivation, 80, 87, 109 (see also Environmental, Sensory and Response deprivation)
  attention, 87
  cages and, 104
  meaning, 87
  mental retardation and, 106
  solitary confinement and, 104
  stereotyped behavior and, 104-6

Performance:
  arousal and, 89-91
Periodicity, 32-33, 35
Phenotype, 113
Phylogeny, 42
Piagetianism, 64-70, 79
Play:
  adaptive significance of, 115
  adult (see Adult play)
  age, 61
  aggression and, 55-57
  American way of life and, 1
  antonym for, 60
    earnest as, 11
    serious as, 11
    work as, 11
  arousal-seeking and, 30-31, 111, 135 (see also Arousal, Arousal level, Arousal-seeking, Stimulus-seeking)
  change and, 82
  characteristics of, 17-20
    in animals, 17-19
    in humans, 19-26
  circular definition of, 81-82
  class differences in, 75
  classical theories of, 23-48 (see also Theory, Classical theories of play)
  cognition and, 64-70
  competence/effectance motive, 30-31, 76, 100-104, 111
  competition and (see Competition)
  constituent behaviors, 20, 101
  creativity and, 21, 127
  criteria for categorizing, 123-27
  culture, 50, 71-74 (see also Learning and Imitation)
  definition of, 2, 9-22, 108-10
  discrimination of work from, 123-27
  dreams and, 59
  education and, 4, 42
  ego, 58
  English language meaning, 10
  evolution and, 113-18
  fatigue and, 28
  games and, 72-74, 75
  handicapped persons and, 146-47
  humor, 1, 21
  hunger, 27
  hypothesis testing and, 132
  importance of, 1-4, 9-10
  indefinable behavior, 20-22
  instinct motive for, 12, 15, 23, 36-49, 45-46
  intrinsic motivation for, 76, 121, 124
  joy, 21
  learning, 4-6, 116-17, 118

Play (cont.)
  management, 2, 26, 119-48
  technology for, 4-6
  managers of, 7
  meaning in:
    English, 10
    occidental cultures, 10
    other languages, 9
  modern theories of play, 80-112 (see also
    Arousal, Arousal-seeking, Stimulus
    seeking and Competence/effec-
    tance)
  necessity of, 110
  nonutilitarian behavior, 9, 27, 76, 80-81,
    83, 88, 107, 109
  "not-play" versus, 10
  playful behavior as, 11, 21
  recapitulation motive for, 13
  recent theories of, 48-79 (see also The-
    ory, recent theories of play)
  recognition:
    by animals, 9
    by humans, 9
  redefinition of, 108-10
  research into, 6-7
  serious behavior, 81
  sex differences in, 75
  spontaneity, 21
  spontaneous behavior as, 15
  stages of, 20
  stereotyped behavior and, 107
  stimulus seeking behavior, 76, 108 (see
    also Arousal, Arousal-seeking, Stim-
    ulus-seeking)
  surplus behavior, 80-81
  surplus energy, 12, 23, 27-33, 46
  theories:
    integration of, 112
  theory, 2
  theory and practice, 6-8, 16
  therapy, 61-64
  variability in, 116
  verbal behavior and, 131
  voluntary behavior and, 13
  work and, 1, 10-11, 33, 108
  work versus, 109-10
Playfulness, 21, 124, 136
  creativity and, 121-22
  criteria for, 121
  inheritance of, 115
Playgrounds, 137-39 (see also Playthings)
  adventure, 139
  attendance at, 137
  characteristics of, 137
  classes of, 138
  design of, 139
  ideal, 137-38

Playgrounds (cont.)
  junk, 140
  leadership, 138
  neighborhood, 138
  one-visit, 138
Playthings, 134-39 (see also Playgrounds
    and Toys)
  arousal created by, 134
  characteristics of good, 136
  children as, 134
  constructional, 137
  definition of, 135
  design of, 136
  real objects as, 135
  selection of, 136
  technological, 137
Pleasure principle, 58, 62, 93, 100 (see also
    Psychoanalytic theory of play, and
    Reinforcement)
  positive affect and, 93
Positive affect, 93-94 (see also Reinforce-
    ment)
Practice theory of play, 41 (see also In-
    stinct, and Preparation theories of
    play)
Predictability, 97, 98, 117 (see also Expec-
    tancy)
Prediction (see Theory, function of)
Preparation, 82-83, 120-22
Preparation theory of play, 23, 40-42, 45,
    47
Preschool, 4
Primary drives, 71, 80-81, 93, 94, 100-101,
    108, 109, 116, 122
Problem-solving, 83
  arousal generated by, 102
  education for, 120-22
  epistemic behavior and, 99-100
  learning and, 83
  play and, 122
  specific responses, 122
Process variables, 129
  definition of, 129
  "press for achievement," 129
    general learning, 129
    language, 129
    play, 129-30
Psychoanalytic theory of play, 49, 57-64,
    79
  competence/effectance and, 101
Publishing industry:
  arousal seeking and the, 143
Punishment (see Reinforcement, negative)
Puritanism, 10, 11

Queueing, 107

Quiescence, 10, 28, 30, 80-81, 94

Racial activities:
developmental stages of, 44
Racial history, 42-44
Racial pursuits, 33, 34
Rainwater, 14
Reality:
play and, 123-27
Rearing environment, 129-30
creativity and, 130
parents and, 130
Rearing patterns, 72-74
different cognitive styles of parents and, 75-76
effects on play, 75-76
sex differences, 75
Recapitulation theory of play, 23, 33, 42-45, 47
Recent theories, characteristics of, 24
Recreation:
goals for, 120
graded task difficulty, 145
learning and, 120
play and, 120-21
programming for adults, 142-44
therapeutic, 146-47
justification for, 147
work and, 142
Recreational activities:
stages of engagement in, 142-43
Recuperation, 33
Rehearsal theory (see Play, motivated by recapitulation)
Reinforcement, 25, 51, 58, 62, 71, 83, 88, 93-94, 101, 115, 117 (see also Consequences, and Contingencies)
activity as, 101
effectance as, 102
exploration as, 88
extrinsic, 5-6
intrinsic, 5-6
locus of control, 123-27
negative, 25, 40
novel responses as, 114
positive, 25, 40-41
primary, 116
secondary, 71, 116
Relaxation theory of play, 23, 33-36, 47, 52
catharsis and, 54
compensation and, 54
Repetitious responding, 132
arousal-seeking and, 102
hypothesis testing, 132

Research:
play and, 7
testing theory, 7
Response deprivation, 28, 29 (see also Environmental, Perceptual, and Sensory deprivation)
Response threshold, 29-30, 35
Retardates, 105, 106
perceptual deprivation and, 106
Reticulate arousal system, 89-91, 101, 105 (see also Brain)
Reward (see Reinforcement)
Rousseau, 4
Running:
as a reward, 31-32 (see also Surplus energy)
Rural culture, 75
acculturation, 75

Schiller, 12, 27
School, 53, 120
Secondary reinforcers, 71 (see also Reinforcement)
Self-stimulation, 86, 90 (see also Epistemic behavior)
fidgeting, 86
day-dreaming, 86
Sensoristasis, 93-94, 95, 96, 97, 105, 109, 110
definition of, 93
drive status of, 110
Sensoristatic drive, 93-94 (see also Sensoristasis, Arousal level, and Stimulus seeking)
learning and, 94
Sensory deprivation, 80, 85, 86, 87, 105, 127, 133 (see also Environmental, Peripheral and Response deprivation)
attitudes, 87
biorhythms, 87
confinement to bed, 146
hallucinations, 87
paradoxical effects of, 105
performance and, 87
physiological functioning, 87
sleep, 87
Sensory-motor hunger, 27
Sesame Street, 4
Skill, games of, 72-74
Sleep, 81, 87, 105
Social interaction, uncertainty inherent in, 98-99
Social play, 139-41
coaction, 140
competition, 139-40

Social play (cont.)
  constraints, others as, 139
  cooperation, 140
  Neumann's criteria and, 139
Souriau, 30
Sport, 33
S-R psychology, 70, 76
Stages:
  developmental, 112, 117
Status variables, 129
  definition of, 129
Stereotyped behavior, 104-7
  alternative activities and, 105, 106
  arousal levels and, 106
  explanation of, 105
  information load of, 106
  information of environment and, 105
  management of, 106
  play and, 107
  self destruction and, 104-5
Stern, 14
Stimuli, 91-93
  classification of, 9
  information content of, 94
  recognition of, 91
Stimulus:
  avoidance, 107
  change, 84-85, 92
  intensity, 92
  meaning, 87
  predictability (see Expectancy)
  seeking, 80-83, 94, 99, 108-9
    covert elements of, 99 (see also Epis-
      temic behavior)
    history of the idea, 83-85
    play as, 108
    selection, 84, 91 (see also Attention)
Strategic games, 72-74
Strategies, 83
Sub-culture, 71
Superego, 58
Surplus energy, 23, 27-33, 45-47
  circularity of the notion, 30-31
  evolution and, 28
  fatigue, 27-29, 33
  health, 29
  hydraulic model of, 31-32
  relaxation, 35
  research on, 31-33
  response deprivation and, 28
Surplus energy theory of play, 23, 27-33,
    45-46, 52 (see also Theory, classical
    theories of play)

Task-completion, 53
Taxonomy, 42

Teachers, 12
Technology:
  leisure time interest in, 44
Teleological error, 41-42
Television, 4
Thematic aggression, 56
Theories of play:
  periodic concern for, 4
Theory:
  acceptance of, 7
  benefits of, 6-8
  classical theories of play, 23-47
    instinct, 23, 36-40, 45-47
    preparation, 23, 40-42, 45, 47
    recapitulation, 23, 33, 42-47
    relaxation, 23, 33-36, 45-47
    surplus energy, 23, 27-33, 45-47
  confirmability of, 26
  definition of play by, 12
  explanation, 48
  function of, 24-26
  practical use of, 7, 26, 119, 147-48
  prediction and, 48
  recent theories of play, 49-79
    cathartic, 49, 54-57, 78
    characteristics of, 49
    cognitive dynamic, 49-50, 65-70, 79
    compensation, 49-54, 78
    generalization, 49-54, 78
    learning, 50, 70-76, 79
    psychoanalytic view, 49, 57-64, 79
  rejection of, 7
  research and, 7
  testing of, 6-7, 26, 27, 77
  usefulness of, 26
Therapeutic effects of play, 59
Thinking, 135 (see also Epistemic behav-
    ior, Cognitive events, Cognitive be-
    havior, and Cognition)
Thorndike, 70
Toys, 4, 55, 63, 75, 131, 137

Uncertainty, 75, 91, 92, 93, 98, 103-4 (see
    also Dissonance, Incongruity, In-
    formation)
  limited capacity for, 95
  optimal level of, 95-96
Urban Culture, 75
  acculturation, 75
Urbanization, 44

Variability:
  inter- and intra-specific, 113
  survival and, 116

Verbal behavior:
  play as, 131
Verbal communication:
  manipulation as, 131
Vigilance, 80, 85, 86, 87

Work, 70, 109
  boring nature, 142

Work (*cont.*)
  criteria for categorizing, 123-27
  extrinsic rewards and, 141
  intrinsic rewards for, 142
  mental, 34
  physical, 34
  play and, 70, 120-27
  play on a continuum with, 109-10

AUTHOR INDEX

Adams, 85
Alexander, 64
Amatruda, 105
Ashby, 114-15, 116
Atkinson, 108
Attneave, 92
Axline, 61

Banks, 122
Barker, 19
Barnett, 16
Beach, 12, 18-19, 31, 36, 39-40
Beaman, 53
Bengtsson, 139
Bennett, 128
Berkowitz, 55, 56, 57
Berkson, 105
Berkun, 101
Berlyne, 1-2, 84, 88, 89, 91, 92, 97, 99, 100, 105, 131
Bernard, 39
Bernstein, 106
Bishop, 52, 75, 129-30, 131
Bloom, 127
Blurton-Jones, 19
Bohrer, 32
Breer, 51
Bronfenbrenner, 128
Buckner, 85
Burgers, 99
Burgess, 56
Butler, 88

Cannon, 96

Chace, 75, 129-30, 131
Cherry, 92
Cofer, 88

Davenport, 105
Dee, 137
Dember, 95, 104, 117
Dennis, 128
Dodson, 107
Dorfman, 64
Duffy, 89, 107

Earl, 95, 104, 117
Edwards, 92
Eifermann, 68-69, 75, 140, 141
Ellis, 32
Erikson, 57, 58, 59, 63, 64
Escalona, 53, 55

Feshbach, 56
Fiske, 9, 89, 107
Flavell, 64, 66, 67
Frankman, 85
Freeman, 80
Freud, A., 64
Freud, 57, 59, 60, 61, 62

Galanter, 64, 84
Gesell, 105
Gewirtz, 128
Gilmore, 23, 61, 62
Glass, 128

Gordon, 129
Gramza, 105
Gray, 128
Green, 57
Groos, 12, 13, 27, 30, 31, 35, 36, 40, 41, 42, 43, 45, 54, 102
Gulick, 14, 43, 44
Gump, 19-20

Hagedorn, 51-52
Hall, 13, 43, 44, 45
Harlow, H. F., 88, 101
Harlow, M. K., 88, 101
Hebb, 82, 86, 91, 98
Hediger, 104-5
Hendrick, 102
Hinde, 9, 33, 35, 89, 91
Hokanson, 56
Hollis, 105
Huizinga, 10, 11, 14
Hull, 24
Hunt, 16, 82
Hurtwood, 139
Hutt, C., 19, 20, 105
Hutt, S., 105

James, 36, 37, 38-39
Jeanrenaud, 97
Jones, 87, 107

Kagan, 101
Kaspar, 32
Kaufman, 105
Keiper, 105
Kelly, 10
Kendon, 74
Kenny, 55, 56
Kerlinger, 24
Kibler, 86
Kimble, 58, 70
Klein, 62, 64
Koch, 105
Kohlberg, 113
Kozelka, 74
Kravitz, 105
Krech, 128

Labowitz, 51-52
Lambie, 128
Leach, 19
Leavitt, 105
Lebo, 64
Lesser, 105

Leuba, 91
Levy, 105
Lewin, 24
Lewis, 75
Lieberman, 21, 121, 137
Liebman, 137
Linder, 3
Lindsley, 93
Linford, 97
Lockard, 113
Locke, 51
Loizos, 18
Lore, 32
Lourie, 105
Lovelace, 97

Mackworth, J., 85, 86
Mackworth, N. H., 85
Maddie, 9, 89, 107
Maier, 64
Mallick, 57
Malmo, 107
Mason, 105, 128
McCandless, 57
McDougall, 37, 38, 84-85
McGrath, 85
Menninger, 55, 57
Menzel, 105
Messer, 75
Meyer, 57, 88, 101
Millar, 21
Miller, G. A., 64, 84
Miller, J. G., 107
Miller, J. O., 128
Mitchell, 10, 12, 14, 33
Montgomery, 88
Morgan, 74
Morris, 40, 81, 82, 107, 133
Moustakas, 64
Murphy, 105

Neumann, 123-26, 129, 136
Nighswander, 57
Nissen, 88

Olson, 105

Painter, 128, 129
Patrick, 14, 33, 34, 54
Pavlov, 83-84, 97
Piaget, 50, 62, 64, 65-68, 69, 70, 125
Poole, 17-18
Popper, 26

Pribram, 64, 84

Ragheb, 112
Redl, 19-20
Roberts, 72, 73, 74
Rogers, 105
Rosenberg, 74
Rosenthal, 105
Rosenzweig, 128

Sackett, 95, 96, 104, 117
Samuels, 89, 107
Sapora, 10, 12, 14, 33
Sargent, 105
Saxon, 105
Schaeffer, 128
Schlosberg, 13, 31, 109
Schoggen, 19-20
Schulman, 32
Schultz, 93, 96, 107
Selye, 29
Spencer, 29-30, 37, 45
Steinman, 2
Stephenson, 99, 143
Stewart, 134
Suedfeld, 87
Sutton-Smith, 68, 72, 73, 74, 75, 131

Teplitz, 105
Thompson, 91, 98, 128
Throne, 32
Tolman, 27-28

Waddington, 96
Wade, G. R., 137
Wade, M. G., 32
Walder, 57-60
Weikart, 128
Welker, 88
White, 30, 58, 83, 100, 102, 103-4
Winter, 134
Witt, 52
Witty, 53
Wolf, 129
Woodworth, 37, 88, 104
Wright, 19

Yerkes, 107

Zipf, 80
Zubek, 87
Zuckerman, 87